KNOWING AND CARING

Philosophical Issues in Social Work

Roberta Wells Imre, Ph.D., ACSW

UNIVERSITY
PRESS OF
AMERICA

LANHAM • NEW YORK • LONDON

Copyright © 1982 by

University Press of America,™ Inc.

4720 Boston Way
Lanham, MD 20706

3 Henrietta Street
London WC2E 8LU England

Library of Congress Cataloging in Publication Data

Imre, Roberta Wells.
    Knowing and caring.

    Bibliography: p.
    Includes index.
    1. Social service–Philosophy. I. Title.
HV40I48   1982   361.3'01   82–20209
ISBN 0–8191–2859–7
ISBN 0–8191–2860–0 (pbk.)

In Memory of My Mother and Father

Acknowledgements

It is not possible to mention specifically the many people who have contributed to the experiences and thought which have produced this book. Much has been learned from clients in various practice settings, from colleagues and fellow students, as well as from teachers.

I would like to express special appreciation to Professors Bruce Lagay and Werner Boehm (in social work) and Bruce Wilshire (in philosophy) at Rutgers University for support and guidance with the doctoral dissertation on which this book is based. Others I would like to thank by name include Emma Quartaro, D.S.W., of the social work faculty at Seton Hall University for her interest and vision of the broader applicability of the ideas presented here; Barbara Molnar for her patience and skill in typing the manuscript; and last but certainly not least my husband, Kaya, for his scientific perspective and moral support.

TABLE OF CONTENTS

INTRODUCTION

Philosophical issues are integrally involved in concepts of knowing and caring in social work education and practice. This study explores the meaning of knowing and the nature of knowledge in social work, emphasizing the integral relationship between the person who knows and that which is known.

At the present time, particularly in academic social work, there is a tendency to consider knowledge to be only that which can be known through empirical science. The emphasis here is upon the need for a broader definition of knowledge--a definition which includes the many aspects of what it means to be a person and what can be known about what is good and valuable in human life. The concept of caring epitomizes this additional dimension of knowing in social work.

For the purpose of this discussion the term social work is used for the most part to refer to the person to person activities which characterize much of social work practice. Most social workers work with people and it is the nature of the knowledge involved in these person to person activities which is the focus here. While the ideas presented may be particularly relevant for direct practice or intervention programs, it should be noted that social policy and planning also require knowledge about what human beings need as well as what society ought to provide.

As with other human activities, social work cannot be separated from the culture in which it has developed. Dominant ways of thinking in a culture tend to be absorbed below the level of awareness and become built into the conventionally accepted knowledge base of a profession in a variety of ways. A deliberate effort is required to question attitudes and assumptions acquired in this way. Ingrained habits of thought are not easily disrupted and a measure of security often must be sacrificed.

The pre-eminent influence of science and technology in American society has been evident for many years. A concomitant diminution of interest in philosophical and theological thought has also occurred during this period. The philosophy of positivism grew out of this cultural situation and is seen here to be a major factor in the

1

tendency in social work to consider knowledge to be only that which is scientific. This definition of knowledge is generally accepted for the most part in an unexamined way.

In the recent literature there are both explicit and implicit assumptions that all valid social work knowledge will ultimately be scientific and that the methods for achieving this are empirical. For example, one article states:

> Occasionally one hears that programs of social work produce outcomes so subtle they cannot be measured but that somehow without them society would be worse off. When the outcome is not measurable, social workers are probably engaging in self delusion.[1]

This trend in thinking can be seen to be a reflection of social work's embeddedness in the culture of its times. It is suggested here that this preoccupation and its philosophical concomitants unnecessarily, even harmfully, narrow the perspectives of a profession traditionally concerned both with alleviating human pain and suffering and with supporting personal growth and development.

The present emphasis in the profession upon effective techniques, quantitatively measured, is understandable in the light of the cultural context in which social work is practiced. However, William Barrett notes that, "The technique cannot produce the philosophy that directs it."[2] The focus on techniques in current social work literature is seen to be rooted in a positivist philosophy, which is considered to be particularly dysfunctional for a profession which needs a philosophy based upon a recognition of what it means to be a human being.

A major emphasis here is upon the importance of knowing in some of the additional dimensions of human life relevant to social work for which scientific methods are not adequate, or even necessarily appropriate. For example, social work will be seen as a moral profession involving ways of thinking and reasoning related to, but different from, those of science. It will also be seen as basically involved with questions relating to meaning and understanding in human life, questions which at times include ultimate concerns.

2

The humanities address these matters in ways which science cannot. Traditionally social work has been viewed as a combination of art and science. Recently, however, there has been a tendency at times to consider art in the profession somewhat apolegetically, as a reference to those aspects of practice which are not yet scientific.[3] In this discussion an effort is made to focus on some of the ways that knowledge to be found in the humanities, with special reference to philosophy and theology as well as art, is essential to the study and practice of social work, which is concerned with human beings for whom results obtained by empirical methods can be useful but are not sufficient.

Two themes, the search for relevant knowledge and the values and moral commitments of the profession, have been recognized whenever efforts have been made to study and define the profession. Efforts to integrate the two, however, have often resulted in more confusion than clarification. It is suggested here that the problem lies in the effort, associated with positivism, to reduce all relevant knowledge to that which is scientific, thus forcing a false dichotomy between knowledge and values.

Modern positivism, with origins in the thought of Descartes in the seventeenth century, is related in its history to the development of science, and thus has been the dominant philosophical influence in the social sciences in this country. Many social scientists believe that positivism makes possible the kind of exactness thought to characterize the physical sciences. Ironically, modern physics, the paradigm of science for the positivists, can be seen to provide illustrations of the inadequacy of this kind of conceptual framework.

Although rarely addressed directly, the assumptions and definitions of positivism are also present in much contemporary social work literature and discourse. The intent here is to call attention to what has been left out of this philosophical position. The emphasis is upon aspects of knowing which include the importance of being a person with capacities to reason, to be enlightened by art in its various forms, to be aware of what is valuable in life, and to confront questions of non-being in the presence of the mystery of being. Relationship and caring are considered to be integral to social work practice and are emphasized because they embody these concerns and represent a moral commitment of the profession, exemplifying a good which can be known.

3

Knowing and caring have been chosen as the primary
focus for this study because they encompass these central issues. Particular emphasis is placed upon other
aspects of knowing in addition to the approaches of empirical science, in an effort to call attention to the
need to develop a more adequate philosophical framework
for this human and humane activity called social work.

Footnotes

[1]Edward Newman and Jerry Turem, "The Crisis of
Accountability," Social Work, 19 (January 1974): 16.

[2]William Barrett, The Illusion of Technique,
(Garden City, New York: Anchor Press/Doubleday, 1978),
p. 105.

[3]See, for example, Scott Briar and Henry Miller,
Problems and Issues in Social Casework (New York:
Columbia University Press, 1971), p. 88.

CHAPTER I

THE NATURE OF SOCIAL WORK

History

Throughout human history there have been people who have sought to help others in need. Probably the most familiar have been those under religious auspices. However, as a speaker at the National Conference of Charities and Corrections in 1892 is quoted as saying regarding the charity organization movement, "Its principles are as old as the mutual needs and mutual obligations of society."[1] What is of interest here, however, is the evolution of the profession of social work as it is found today, particularly in the United States.

One of the primary antecedents of social work was the charity organization movement which began in England and was later adapted to conditions in the United States. The charity organization societies were originally an effort to respond in an organized fashion to the needs of obviously indigent and poverty stricken people in industrial society. The first such society in the United States was established in Buffalo in 1877.[2]

Earlier efforts to deal with the problems of the poor in the United States can be found in the Society for the Prevention of Pauperism in New York City in 1817, which a few years later devoted its resources to the prevention of juvenile delinquency, and the various Associations for Improving the Condition of the Poor, beginning in 1843. However, the roots of social work, especially those activities which came to be called casework, can be most clearly seen in the charity organization movement which provided the stimulus for the development of the profession as currently practiced. The Reverend Gurteen, the founder of the Charity Organization Society in Buffalo, brought from England a knowledge of the program which had been developed by the London Charity Organization Society. This approach was adapted to conditions in Buffalo and later to other cities.

The charity organization societies began in this country in the period of social upheaval which followed the civil war and the subsequent depression--a period in which efforts to aid the poor were disorganized and without safeguards either for those in need or those who would aid. Beggars were common and there was no way to assure help to those unable or unwilling to beg.

Margaret E. Rich, who was active in the family service field from its earliest days in this country, said in her history of that movement:

> Year by year there was an increase in the number of people receiving relief from the city 'poor' department, in the number of tramps who went from house to house and beggars who accosted people on the street.[3]

It is of the very nature of social work that it must operate within the cultural context of the current historical period. Because of this, the profession in its history can be seen to reflect many of the conflicts and inconsistencies of its time. From the beginning and throughout its relatively short history social work has been influenced by, and at times has been able to influence, the current political, economic, religious, and social thought.

The founders of the charity organization society movement were motivated by the desire to find ways to help those in economic need. As children of their own historical period, however, they sought a solution in terms of the class structure of the time in which noblesse oblige, and the resulting paternalism, was an important element. The rich were seen as having an obligation to aid and to be benevolent toward the poor. In addition to the philanthropic motivation, there was also the more self serving purpose to prevent further social disorganization.[4] The hope was that this approach would defuse the growing social unrest associated with the exploitation of labor and the desperately inadequate living conditions seen most clearly in the increasingly crowded cities.

The organizational plan of the societies included those who administered the programs and the volunteers, who were called friendly visitors, and who were expected to become friends and advisors to the poor families. These early ventures met with many difficulties. For example, there was an ineffectual effort to separate the actual relief given from the services of the visitors. These problems were rooted in the impracticality of trying to help people in dire need without first attending to basic sustenance requirements.

In these early days there was a continuing struggle with the problems of providing adequate assistance to meet physical needs while also seeking ways to help people become self sustaining. The charity organiza-

6

tion societies were private, voluntary agencies in contrast to publicly financed welfare assistance. The development of both types of agencies was intertwined and became more clearly separated as government took over more social programs providing economic assistance. These organizational efforts to provide broader public programs were supported by the charity organization societies.[5]

A basic criticism of these early voluntary agencies has been related to the effort to divide those in need into the worthy and the unworthy, the latter to be assisted by the public agenices. It is important to note that the root of this kind of moralistic discrimination was to be found in the socio-cultural situation. Later, as the political and attitudinal climate changed, there were efforts to build social responsibility into the law and thus into the public agencies. The social security laws and changes in federal support for public assistance to include categorical aid (to mothers and dependent children, the physically disabled, and the elderly) were designed to provide needed help on the basis of right or entitlement and were supported by what by then had become social work organizations.

Applications of the concept of entitlement, that all people have the right to the resources necessary for a decent life and that society must make these resources available to those who need them, has fluctuated with changing social and political conditions. Perhaps most often honored by way of the social security system, this concept has rarely been implemented without ambivalence in public assistance programs. Those social workers who are called caseworkers have often been caught in this societal ambivalence.

Growing concomitantly with the charity organization societies was the settlement movement which led to the development of the social work specialty later called group work.[6] This movement had a number of emphases different from those involved in the charity organization societies. Staff, including college students volunteering their services, were expected to live in the area served. The recipients were chiefly working class and some settlement workers actively supported the growing organized labor movement. Services were primarily educational and recreational with increasing involvement in efforts to improve social conditions thorugh social action and legislation. The settlement group had early ties to the colleges and universities then in existence and there was interest and mutual exchange with the developing social sciences.

The history of the charity organizations in regard to higher education was somewhat different from that of the settlements. There was an early recognition of the need for more knowledge. This took the form of emphasizing record keeping, narrative and statistical, and the sponsorship of institute and educational programs for workers. Later affiliations with colleges and universities were developed whereby the schools provided academic content, with the agencies (then predominantly charity organization societies) providing the practical experience later called fieldwork.

Contemporary views of the history of social work differ in their emphases and interpretations. Germain believes that history accounts for what she sees as a continuing argument within the profession over individual treatment versus social action to improve conditions.[7] On the other hand other historians, as well as some of the early writers in the field, emphasize the degree to which social workers were actively concerned about environmental factors seen to be damaging to the people with whom they worked. A good example, still relevant, can be seen in the following paragraph from Mary Richmond's Friendly Visiting Among the Poor, published in 1899.

It is well to realize that much of the political corruption of our large cities may be traced to the simple fact that the poor man is like ourselves: he follows the leaders personally known to him, and to whom he is personally known. He is sometimes a venal voter, but more often he is only an ignorant voter, who, while innocently following the man that has taken the trouble to do him a favor or to be socially agreeable to him, is handicapping himself and his children with dirty streets, an unsanitary home, an overcrowded school, an insufficient water supply, blackmailing officials, and all those other abuses of city government which press with peculiar hardship upon the poor. The question of municipal reform is inextricably connected with any effort to improve the condition of the poor in their homes, and no charity worker can afford to ignore this connection.[8]

Later, in Social Diagnosis, Richmond said in her first chapter:

Mass betterment and individual betterment are interdependent, however, social reform and social case work of necessity progressing together. This fundamental truth will appear repeatedly as the present discussion of social diagnosis advances.[9]

Social work as a profession grew eventually to include a combination of approaches to human suffering rooted in poverty and other social conditions. Contributions to this development came from several different directions including charity organization societies and the settlements. Social work now encompasses a variety of modes of practice currently subsumed under such headings as administration, community organization, social planning, and social policy, as well as casework and group work.

As indicated earlier, attention is focused here particularly on those activities which involve direct person to person help. Despite doubts expressed in the social work literature regarding the contemporary relevance and/or effectiveness of much of this direct practice, this aspect still attracts a large number of the students studying social work, and remains an important activity in the lives of many people.

People affected by these activities may be individual participants in services such as practitioners and clients, or others less directly involved. One of the primary values of this aspect of social work can be seen to be the affirmation of the importance of the individual in a highly industrialized, technological society. It is one way to help counter the isolation and alienation experienced by many persons in this kind of world.

Current Situation

Direct practice in social work, which is emphasized here, constitutes a profession whereby individuals with special training seek to help other individuals with problems they experience in their daily living. It is a person to person effort to help people find resources, internal and external, to cope with these difficulties. Since human beings are essentially social beings and interdependent, this kind of helping is concerned with the social relationships of people.

Some of these services focus on providing, or aiding people in finding, concrete services. Other pro-

9

grams are involved primarily in helping people in their relationships with one another--in intimate ways such as in family life and in the broader social world of organizations and institutions which are characteristic of life in modern western civilization.

Social workers are to be found in many different settings and are supported either by public or private, voluntary resources. In some places, most notably in the judicial system, as well as others, such workers can be seen to have a social control function. Some authors have suggested that this function is its primary purpose, acknowledged or unacknowledged.[10] While recognizing that social work is sometimes used in this way, the perspective presented here is that the social worker has a broader function of affirming the intrinsic worth of the individual person and his entitlement to help if it is needed. This affirmation is implicit in the way the person to person services are offered.

Providing services to people in need, in a manner which affirms their common humanity and seeks to enable them to develop their own potential abilities to find solutions to their problems, can be seen to be in accord with social work tradition as found in the writings of such major figures as Hamilton, Hollis, Perlman, Towle, and others.[11]

Since the earliest days of the charity organization societies there has been a recognition of the need for more knowledge in the complex task of helping people. The early literature indicates how the recognition of the need to know more about people, individually and socially, led eventually to the establishment of schools of social work and to specific educational expectations for casework practitioners. While degree requirements have varied from time to time, there has been a consistent recognition of the need for skilled knowledge in the history of the profession.

Efforts to deal with education for social work in an organized fashion resulted in the development of the Association of Training Schools for Professional Social Work in 1919. In 1952, after a number of changes over the years, the present Council on Social Work Education (CSWE) came into being. This Council is now the accrediting body for schools of social work.

A CSWE statement, "Curriculum Policy for the Master's Degree Program in Graduate Schools of Social Work," says:

10

The professional curriculum for social work
draws broadly and selectively from the humanities, from other professions and scientific
disciplines, as well as from the knowledge and
experience developed by social work. Application of this content to social work involves
ethical as well as scientific commitment. The
study and analysis of ethical considerations
is an important component of social work education.[12]

This statement indicates four sources of knowledge
which are important to this discussion of knowing in
social work--the humanities, scientific disciplines,
other professions, and social work experience. In
addition, knowledge of the self, oneself and others,
will also be seen to be vital to a discussion of knowing in social work. The dual focus on ethical and
humanitarian as well as scientific commitments in this
statement are themes which recur throughout the present
discussion.

Footnotes

[1]Margaret E. Rich, A Belief in People, (New York:
Family Service Association of America, 1956), p. vi.

[2]Ibid., and Encyclopedia of Social Work, 17th Ed.,
s.v. "Charity Organization Society," by Vera S. Lewis,
p. 96.

[3]Rich, A Belief in People, p. 3.

[4]Kathleen Woddroofe, From Charity to Social Work,
(London: Routledge & Kegan Paul, 1968), pp. 50-51.

[5]Rich, A Belief in People, p. 66.

[6]Encyclopedia of Social Work, 17th Ed. s.v. "Settlements: History," by Alan F. Davis, and "Social Group
Work: The Organizational and Environmental Approach,"
by Paul D. Glasser and Charles D. Garbin.

Carel Germain and Alex Gitterman, <u>The Life Model of Social Work Practice</u>, (New York: Columbia University Press, 1980), pp. 347-365.

[8]Mary E. Richmond, <u>Friendly Visiting Among the Poor</u>, (1899; reprint ed., Montclair, New Jersey: Patterson Smith Edition, 1969), pp. 20-21.

[9]Mary E. Richmond, <u>Social Diagnosis</u>, (New York: Russell Sage Foundation, 1917; reprint ed., New York: The Free Press, 1965), p. 25.

[10]The complexity of this issue is recognized by Harold Lewis, in "Toward a Planned Approach in Social Work Research," in <u>Future of Social Work Research</u>, ed. David Fanshel (Washington, D.C.: National Association of Social Workers, 1980), p. 25.

[11]Gordon Hamilton, <u>Theory and Practice of Social Case Work</u>, (New York: Columbia University Press, 1940); Florence Hollis, <u>Casework, A Psychosocial Theory</u>, (New York: Random House, 1964); Helen Harris Perlman, <u>Social Casework, A Problem Solving Process</u>, (Chicago: University of Chicago Press, 1957);Charlotte Towle, <u>Helping</u>, ed. Helen Harris Perlman, (Chicago: University of Chicago Press, 1969).

[12]Council on Social Work Education, "Curriculum Policy for the Master's Degree Program in Graduate Schools of Social Work," n.d.

CHAPTER II

OF SOCIAL WORK PHILOSOPHY

Social work has an uneasy relationship with philosophy even though philosophical issues are integrally involved in social work practice. There is a tendency in academic social work to suggest that most relevant knowledge is, or should be, scientific and that values are essentially preferences.[1] When the word philosophy is used in social work it usually refers to values, and there is little or no recognition of knowing and ways of knowing as basically philosophical issues. Even though, as the CSWE statement indicates, ethical commitments are considered vital to the practice of social work, the intrinsic relationship of ethics and problems concerning the nature of knowledge to philosophy has rarely been acknowledged.

Schools of social work all affirm their commitment to social work values[2] and most assume that congruent philosophical content is presented in courses within the standard curriculum. There are very few schools which offer any specific courses using philosophical resources, although this is beginning to change. There is a developing interest in the field in ethical issues including the passage of a new code of ethics by the National Association of Social Workers and an increasing awareness that this is a more complex subject than previously recognized. The latest edition of the Encyclopedia of Social Work does not include philosophy, or even values, as topics, although it does contain articles on ethics and the history of basic ideas in relation to social welfare. In addition, professional journals in this country have not given much attention to the relevance of philosophy to social work. Some articles and a few books have been published with reference to specific philosophical positions such as humanism or existentialism.[3] In the principal journal for social work education there have been occasional articles dealing with the philosophical question of knowledge, particularly scientific knowledge and values.[4] There is also a recent comprehensive article by Heineman on the limitations of the philosophy of logical empiricism for social work research.[5]

Occasional authors, for example, Helen Perlman, mention the influence of the American philosopher, John Dewey, who was at one point involved in the early settlement movement. There are also occasional incidental references to other philosophers, but rarely any direct

13

attention to philosophical thought. There are some exceptions. John Rawls' volume on justice[6] has been discussed in the literature,[7] and in some courses. In addition, there are two quite recent articles on ethics in social work by Reamer in which he utilizes a variety of philosophical sources, most notably the writings of Alan Gewirth.[8]

There has been somewhat more activity in Great Britain with reference to social work and philosophy, where there have been some efforts to bring philosophers and social workers together to think about issues in social work, usually with reference to particular aspects of society or of practice.[9] While the Hastings Center in this country has recently included social work in its study of professional ethics[10] the broader topic of philosophy and social work for the most part has not been given this kind of interdisciplinary attention in the United States.

While this summary cannot be considered to be a comprehensive survey of references to philosophy in the social work literature, it does demonstrate that attributed philosophical thinking is not common or in any way systematic.

That social workers are often not aware of philosophical elements in their practice is evident in a doctoral dissertation by Tokayer in which he sought to study the social work philosophies of a sample of thirty-four casework practitioners as they themselves viewed this dimension of their work.

He found that:

None of the respondents could state with any degree of conviction that they had a social work philosophy. Most respondents pondered the question and would not make a definitive statement whether positive or negative. It is nonetheless significant that common to most respondents was the notion that they did not have a social work philosophy, even at the conclusion of the interview. Some respondents insisted that they could not encompass the "whole profession," they could only talk about their own social work philosophy. Some respondents affirmed that they had a philosophy, but were not sure whether their philosophy was a personal one, a religious one, or a social work philosophy.[11]

Occasionally philosophy is found in the social work literature in the commonly used sense of what is often called a personal philosophy of life. This usage is often related to the idea of values of personal preferences and may well be a part of the confusion experienced by the participants in the study.

The summaries of Tokayer's interviews with caseworkers indicate, however, that practice is integrally involved with philosophical issues, including those related to knowing and to what is known. In his review of social work literature Tokayer also noted important gaps in the attention given to the question of social work philosophy by those concerned with studying education and practice.

There has been no recent major study dealing with the dimensions of social work practice. Most discussions refer to the Working Definition of Social Work Practice developed by the National Association of Social Workers in 1956. This study defined social work practice, as of all professions, as a "constellation of values, purpose, sanction, knowledge, and method" and the distinguishing mark for social work as the "particular content and configuration of this constellation."[12]

Using this description of social work Tokayer concluded that social work philosophy is:

> ...That which serves to explain the phenomenon with which social workers are confronted in their work, and it serves as a guide for their activities as social workers.

He identified two processes involved as:

> the reordering of existing knowledge, attitudes, values, beliefs, and theories for a new use-- one that is conducive to facilitate social work practice; and/or the development or creation of new knowledge, attitudes, values, beliefs, or theories crucial and particular to the practice of social work.[13]

Tokayer's study was designed to explore social work philosophy "as it inheres in the practice of social work and is carried by the social work practitioner."[14] The study has particular relevance for the discussion here in that all the social workers in the sample were experienced practitioners.

The summaries of the interviews with the caseworkers focused on three primary questions: "What is your social work philosophy? How did you develop your social work philosophy? and What is its role in practice?"

Some of the confusions within the profession are mirrored in the summaries of the interviews in this study. For example, some respondents refer to a philosophy or a religious attitude as abstract and idealistic in contrast to actual behavior on the person to person level, reflecting a kind of conventional stereotype of philosophy and religion.

Historically there has sometimes been a tendency to suggest that social workers are "doers" somehow in contrast to theoreticians or "thinkers." The material in these interviews, plus observations from personal casework experience, indicate that this is an inaccurate and unduly limited view of the social work process, which involves an integration of various kinds of knowledge, information, and theories, beliefs and convictions. All these aspects are part of the person of the social worker as the person of the client, with similar complexity, is confronted and related to.

Social workers have dynamic philosophies, but they are not at home with the language of philosophy. This creates a kind of vacuum in conceptualization which may account for difficulties in assessing the implications of the philosophies of other disciplines whose content is relevant to casework--a difficulty that will be noted later with reference to positivism and the utilization of material from other disciplines.

The summaries of Tokayer's interviews indicate clearly a perception on the part of the caseworkers interviewed that knowledge and use of self are vital parts of their practice. At least one respondent said, "I am the only tool I have."

The kind of knowing needed by social workers in direct practice is personal knowledge--i.e., not only recognition of the essential involvement of the person in knowledge (in the ways described by Polanyi to be discussed later), but also the knowledge of oneself as a person. For practitioners this means an integration of the various kinds of knowing that enable the worker to focus on the other and to reach out as one human being to another. It can be described as the knowing use of self for the benefit of the other. The philosophical importance of this aspect of practice is rarely recognized and seldom explored. For example, one of Tokayer's conclusions states:

> Furthermore, it may be surmised that social
> workers believe that that which undergirds,
> underpins, and gives direction to their
> practice has less to do with a conception of
> practice than it does with a conception of
> the nature of man--what a person is and what
> a person needs.[15]

It was difficult for those caseworkers interviewed by Tokayer to express in the necessary abstractions the philosophical meaning and importance of what they do. It may be that the very process of casework in a way inhibits this kind of mental activity. Perhaps the reason for this is related to the nature of thinking as discussed by Hannah Arendt.

> For thinking's chief characteristic is that it
> interrupts all doing, all ordinary activities
> no matter what they happen to be. Whatever
> the fallacies of the two-world theories might
> have been, they arose out of genuine experiences.
> For it is true that the moment we start thinking
> on no matter what issue we stop everything else,
> and this everything else, again whatever it may
> happen to be, interrupts the thinking process;
> it is as though we moved into a different world.
> Doing and living in the most general sense of
> inter homines esse, "being among my fellow-men"
> --the Latin equivalent for being alive--
> positively prevents thinking. As Valery once
> put it: 'Tantôt je suis, tantôt je pense,'
> now I am, now I think.[16]

In the present discussion it seems more useful to substitute the word reflecting for thinking as used by Arendt. Social workers may have particular difficulty in reflecting on their professional practice in the midst of doing it.

Direct practice involves an intense kind of mental activity, even when overt activity is minimal. Most practitioners come to understand that at times the "being there" is what is important and that more phys- ical activity is not always either required or helpful. It calls for the disciplined use of self, while in the presence of another on whom one's attention is focused. The quality of social work is very much that of "being among my fellow-men." Reflection on the other hand requires a kind of withdrawal into the self-or at least a focusing on one's own thoughts, and a resistance to the distractions involved in interaction with others.

Most social work educators would accept as also applicable to their field what Broudy describes in seeking a rationale for a liberal education. He says:

> It may seem odd to be searching for such a rationale when, ever since Aristotle, everyone has 'known' that beyond specialized training for an occupation there is education for man as man, that is, cultivation of those powers man shares with no other species; clear thinking, enlightened cherishing, and humane judgment.[17]

There is a tendency in this field of social work, however, to believe that the only clear thinking is scientific and that virtues such as enlightened cherishing and humane judgment are either not appropriate subjects for direct attention or that they will take care of themselves, somehow flowing naturally from the content of the curriculum. The intent here is to show that the cultivation of these powers is an appropriate and necessary philosophical activity in social work.

Footnotes

[1]See, for example, William E. Gordon, "Knowledge and Values: Their Distinction and Relationship in Clarifying Social Work Practice," Social Work 10 (July 1965):32-39.

[2]Concerns about values have been discussed at various times in the social work literature in the United States. See, for example, Werner W. Boehm, "The Role of Values in Social Work," The Jewish Social Service Quarterly XXVI (June 1950):429-438: Muriel Pumphrey, The Teaching of Values and Ethics in Social Work Education, Vol. XIII, Project Report of the Curriculum Study (New York: Council on Social Work Education, 1959); and, more recently, Charles P. Levy, Values and Ethics for Social Work Practice (Washington, D.C.: National Association of Social Workers, 1979).

[3]See, for example, Donald F. Krill, Existential Social Work, (New York: Free Press, 1978); Elizabeth L. Saloman, "Humanistic Values and Social Casework," Social Casework 48 (January 1967):26-32; Robert B. Sinsheimer, "The Existential Casework Relationship," Social Casework 50 (February 1969):67-73.

[4]See Hans S. Falck, "Twentieth Century Philosophy of Science and Social Work Education," Journal of Education for Social Work 6 (Spring 1970):21-27; Charles S. Levy, "The Value Base of Social Work," Journal of Education for Social Work 9 (Winter 1973):34-42; Henry S. Maas, "Social Work Knowledge and Social Responsibility," Journal of Education for Social Work 4 (Spring 1968):37-48; Joseph L. Vigilante, "Between Values and Science: Education for a Profession During a Moral Crisis or Is Proof Truth?," Journal of Education for Social Work 10 (Fall 1974):107-115.

[5]Martha Brunswick Heineman, "The Obsolete Scientific Imperative in Social Work Research," Social Service Review 55 (September 1981):371-397.

[6]John Rawls, A Theory of Justice (Cambridge, Massachusetts: Harvard University Press, 1971).

[7]See Harold Lewis, "Morality and the Politics of Practice," Social Casework 53 (July 1972):404-417; and Harold Lewis, Review of A Theory of Justice by John Rawls, in Social Work 18 (July 1973):113-116.

[8]Frederic J. Reamer, "Ethical Content in Social Work," Social Casework 61 (November 1980):531-540; Frederic J. Reamer, "Fundamental Ethical Issues in Social Work: An Essay Review," Social Service Review 53 (June 1979):229-243.

[9]See, for example, Noel Timms and David Watson, eds., Philosophy in Social Work (Boston: Routledge & Kegan Paul, 1978), and other volumes in the International Library of Welfare and Philosophy series of the same publisher. See also Values in Social Work, Social Work Curriculum Study (London, England: Central Council for Education and Training in Social Work, 1976).

[10]Frederic G. Reamer and Marcia Abramson, The Teaching of Social Work Ethics (Hastings-on-Hudson, New York: The Hastings Center, 1982).

[11]Norman Tokayer, "What Social Work Practitioners Conceive as Social Work Philosophy in the Nature of Their Practice," (Ph.D. Dissertation, University of Pennsylvania, 1976), p. 92.

[12]Harriett M. Bartlett, "Toward Clarification and Improvement of Social Work Practice," Social Work 3 (April 1958):3-9.

[13]Tokayer, p. 30.

[14]Ibid., p. 33.

[15]Ibid., p. 216.

[16]Hannah Arendt, "Thinking and Moral Considerations: A Lecture," Social Research 38, (Autumn, 1971): 423.

[17]Harry S. Broudy, "Tacit Knowing as a Rationale for Liberal Education," in Education and Values, ed. Douglas Sloan (New York: Teachers College Press, 1980): p. 50.

CHAPTER III

RELATIONSHIP TO PHILOSOPHY IN GENERAL

As indicated in the previous section there is confusion within the social work profession as to what is meant by philosophy. Social workers are not alone in this perplexity. There are many definitions of philosophy, for example, the American heritage Dictionary of the English Language gives twelve and the Oxford Universal Dictionary gives nine.[1]

For the purpose of this discussion, philosophy will be used generally to apply to reflection about underlying assumptions and their meaning and implications in education and practice. It will be used in the sense described by Gallagher when he says:

> Philosophy does not consist so much in a set of
> formulated answers as it does in the entering
> into a certain kind of question. Philosophy is
> the awakening out of acceptance, just as Plato
> emphasized for his own purposes in the myth of
> the cave.[2]

The approach here will utilize philosophical resources which can be seen to illuminate the issues involved in social work.

The branch of philosophy called epistemology, which deals generally with the nature of knowledge, can be considered to be most directly relevant to this discussion. However, it also appears that knowing in general, and specifically in social work, is integrally involved with questions about being and meaning in human life, thus reaching also into the areas of ontology. These concerns are basically those of metaphysics, which includes both epistemology and ontology, and represents the broadest kind of inquiry into, and reflection upon, meaning and value in human life. In the subsequent discussion, however, an effort will be made where possible to avoid the word metaphysical because of the tendency within the social work profession to react reflexively, as if the word applied to otherworldly concerns in contrast to the here and now. The purpose of this discussion is to seek to deepen perspectives on the nature of social work and to awaken the profession to the questions implicit in the meaning of knowing as it applies to social work practice.

Philosophy, which is not a unified discipline, encompasses a variety of approaches and attitudes. The underlying questions about why anything is, what the nature of the world is, and who or what human beings are, have occupied thinkers for centuries. Western civilization, the context in which social work is to be found, is relatively new when viewed in the light of human history. The scientific thought and associated technology so evident in the modern world have arisen only in the last few centuries--and have notably accelerated in the twentieth century.

Philosophical thought has been very much involved with the developments of science and technology. Many of the most influential philosophers of the eighteenth and nineteenth centuries were also mathematicians and scientists, and the history of science and philosophy are intertwined. Certain strands of this history are especially important for this discussion and are discussed later under specific headings.

Here, however, it is important to note that questions of scientific truth are appropriate philosophical issues. In fields such as social work this is not always recognized. Social work literature tends to accredit science as the source of truth, or certainty, without sufficient consideration of questions about the nature of truth. Many kinds of systems have been built on assertions about truth, but none has been found which is so convincing as to engender universal acceptance.

The search for truth is closely related to definitions of knowledge. It is generally accepted that human beings know and that what is known can be considered knowledge. The difficulty arises with the recognition that what is called knowledge in one period of time can sometimes subsequently be demonstrated to be error. If knowledge can be found to be in error, the inquiry is driven back again to questions of what is truth, and what are the criteria for deciding what is true. It seems to be the fate of human thought that as soon as someone has apparently contained the question and pointed to answers, others come along and shake up the premises.

Bronowski says of the present situation in science:

...all our descriptions of all nature carry a penumbra of uncertainty. In trying to formalize a rule, we look for truth, but what we

22

find is knowledge, and what we fail to find is certainty.[3]

A need for certainty has been a human preoccupation throughout the centuries. It is closely related to doubt and what can be doubted. Descartes' prodigious effort to confront doubt, and to discover what it was possible to know with certainty culminated in the phrase, Cogito, ergo sum, ("I think, therefore I am"), which had profound implications for the development of thought. Descartes in the early seventeenth century reasoned from a position of faith in a God who would not deceive, or allow him to be deceived, and arrived at a picture of a created world of matter in motion governed by mathematical principles--machine like and operated by God.

This was the world Descartes could perceive clearly and distinctly--an external world of the really real. It was possible, he thought, to mislead the mind, about which little could be asserted beyond the self consciousness of the Cogito. Thus there was established a dualism which still haunts the modern world--and notably influences thinking in the social sciences and hence in social work. This is the doctrine that the really real world is objective and external to the observer and that all else is subjective and quite possibly illusory.

This thinking, which was further developed by Descartes' philosophical successors, including Locke and Hume, underlies the positivist philosophy which is dominant in the social sciences,[4] and in other areas of American culture.[5] The specific philosophy of positivism will be discussed in detail in a later chapter. For the present, however, the following quotation from Barrett is relevant.

Our civilization has been described by one commentator as the triumph of the fact. And the fact is a fact for us the more physical, the more 'objective,' the more measurable it is. 'Facts and figures'--the pairing in this phrase is significant--the computer and the I.B.M. card, are considered more real than the intangibles of personal existence. In this sense-- and we had all better recognize it quickly-- our civilization is, or is tending to become, de facto positivistic; and in consequence, positivism is the philosophy endemic to our present

climate of opinion, all the more powerfully
operative when it is unconscious.[6]

The paradigm for this view of the world as objective and out there, a view which is conventionally
thought to be the perspective of science, is mathematical physics. In physics, however, with the advent of
quantum mechanics and the theory of relativity, it became clear that this view was oversimplified and to
that extent inaccurate. The scientist's participation
in his experiments must be taken into account. He is
not able to stand outside and study an objective world
totally apart from himself and unaffected by his activities. Some attention will be given later to the ways
in which the philosophy of science has moved beyond
these artificially imposed boundaries characteristic
of a positivist point of view.

In this discussion it is important to note that
within philosophy there are of course a wealth of differing points of view, past and present. In some respects
these other points of view can be seen to be embattled
in a society in which a scientific technology predomi-
nates. The present discussion will draw upon some of
these other points of view. The intent is to indicate
a potentially broader philosophical base for social
work in which scientific disciplines and the humanities
are seen not as antagonists but as mutually concerned
with a search for truth--where the complexity and the
universality of the search are recognized, along with
the acceptance that no definitive answer acceptable to
all has ever been found or likely ever will be.

Footnotes

[1] The American Heritage Dictionary of the English
Language (1969), and The Oxford Universal Dictionary,
rev. ed. (1955), s.v. "Philosophy."

[2] Kenneth T. Gallagher, The Philosophy of Knowledge
(New York: Sheed and Ward, 1964), p. 6.

[3] J. Bronowski, The Identity of Man, quoted in David
Beres, "Certainty: A Failed Quest?," Psychoanalytic
Quarterly XLIX (1980), p. 12.

[4]Donald P. Warwick, The Teaching of Ethics in the Social Sciences (Hastings-on-Hudson, New York: The Hastings Center, 1980).

[5]See, for example, Barrett, The Illusion of Technique; Alston Chase, "Skipping Through College, Reflections on The Decline of Liberal Arts Education," The Atlantic, September 1978, pp. 33-40; Douglas Sloan, ed., Education and Values (New York: Teachers College Press, 1980).

[6]William Barrett, "The Twentieth Century in Its Philosophy," Commentary 4 (April 1962): 327.

CHAPTER IV

CULTURAL BACKGROUND - SIGNIFICANT CHARACTERISTICS

Science and Technology

For the purpose of the discussion here two related cultural characteristics can be identified as having particular importance in both the development of, and current theory and practice in, social work. The pivotal factor as the earlier discussion suggests is the predominance of science and technology in modern culture. The other characteristic of relevance here is a growing interest of many professions in significant moral issues associated with other societal changes.

The technology which modern science has made possible has profoundly changed the way life is lived in the western world. The term Industrial Revolution was first used by Toynbee to refer to the period beginning in the mid eighteenth century. The influence of a technology based upon scientific advances is evident in the following statement dealing with the period of roughly from 1750 to the beginning of the twentieth century.

> Four factors brought about an extraordinary increase in the means by which man was able to control his environment. They were: new machinery by which man's productive capacity has been increased to an almost unlimited extent; new kinds of power to motivate the machinery; new methods of extracting and using metals, which industry now had need of in ever increasing amounts, and the application of new discoveries in pure science to the technological needs of industry, thus bringing about greater production, new occupations and new wares.[1]

The importance of new technology in these developments is obvious. In addition, there was an associated shift of populations from rural to urban areas, intensifying social problems in the cities.

More recently, developments in modern physics have led to what has been called the atomic age. Extraordinary changes, in both scientific thought and in society have resulted from these discoveries. The effects have been at once both useful and supportive of life and at the same time potentially dangerous and threatening to human survival.

With the growth of scientific thought and evidence of the way it can lead to new, previously undreamed of technologies, confidence in science, and its capacities to understand nature and expand the dimensions of what human beings could know and do, grew. In this climate an attitude which came to be called scientism arose and flourished. Scientism is the belief that only the methods of empirical science can discover what is true and that these methods are applicable to all areas of human life. Scientism is also related to a positivistic definition of knowledge. Many scientists themselves have been critical of these exaggerated claims. For example, Holton describes scientism as "an addiction to science." He says:

Among the signs of scientism are the habit of dividing all thought into two categories, up-to-date scientific knowledge and nonsense; the view that the mathematical sciences and the large nuclear laboratory offer the only permissible models for successfully employing the mind or organizing effort; and the identification of science with technology.[2]

The exaggerated assessment of science represented by scientism is also related to historical conflicts between the discoveries of scientists and the institutional church. At times the church openly persecuted, or prosecuted, early scientists whose work contradicted a church doctrine, for example the treatment of Galileo in the seventeenth century.[3]

Conflicts between scientific perspectives and the prevalent views of the relationships of man, the earth, and the cosmos, contributed to the growth of a belief that science pointed the way to truth, in opposition to religion which was assumed to be dogmatic and coercive and hence closed to the evidence of new discoveries. This limited view of religion as identified with a conservative institution, coupled with confidence in scientific techniques, has made it unfashionable to consider certain aspects of human life as appropriate areas for academic study.

In the subsequent discussion the ways in which social work has been affected by these cultural attitudes is elaborated. For the present, the human tendency to try to finalize a particular attitude should be noted. For example, the physicist, David Bohm says:

> As the expression of reason in thought and language is repeated, it tends to become relatively fixed in terms of what may be called 'formal logic.' It is this that constitutes the main core of our ordinary thinking. Such thinking is, as we have said earlier, both necessary and useful in practical life. However, it has to be noted that it also tends to combine with fixed emotional and social responses to produce rigid grooves and closed compartments, with an attendant hubris that attributes final truth to whatever may be the prevailing general notions. And thus the formal logical approach, developed into habit and routine, has generally become a major barrier to further insight.[4]

Moral and Ethical Issues

The second cultural factor considered here as having particular relevance to social work is the moral and ethical climate in the United States. This climate has been profoundly influenced by science and technological developments--often in ways which are not immediately apparent. As indicated, history reveals conflicts between scientific discoveries and the doctrines of the institutional church, seeming to justify an identification of religion with dogma and coercion, resulting in a lessening of religious influence. (There is of course the phenomenon of the growth of various sects. The concern in this discussion, however, will be with the effects of the apparent conflict between religion and science in the academic disciplines influencing social work.) The philosophy of positivism and the related scientistic attitudes have also contributed to confusion about the grounds for value judgments and professional decisions with ethical import.

Accompanying the growth of faith in science has been an associated decline in emphasis upon the humanities in general. This influence has had pronounced effects in the academic world with increased pressure for vocationally oriented programs and less emphasis upon the liberal arts with their qualitative concerns and value judgments.

Positivism also led to a lessening of interest in understanding moral issues which were relegated to a

29

realm of personal preference for which no evaluative standards were to be considered necessary, or even possible.

The tendency to view science as the final arbiter of truth, combined with the tremendous changes in the physical accoutrements of life resulting from technological growth and development, have also contributed to the cultural trend toward secularization and materialism. The theologian, Albert Outler, in a recent article which received attention in the New York Times and other news media, states that for modern man "the demoralization of the human is the bitter fruit of a loss of the sacred."[5] Associated with the climate thus engendered is the growth of a kind of socially fostered narcissism encouraging self indulgence and self aggrandizement. This kind of materialistic individualism can be seen in the popular literature in which the Dale Carnegies of one generation have been followed by a plethora of authors suggesting ways to enhance the self--by dieting, improving sexual prowess, or achieving financial success while the rest of the world collapses.

Some writers have associated these trends with the growth of what sociologists have called anomie--confusion and normlessness on a societal level. On an individual level the person may experience, consciously or unconsciously, a despair of meaning.

Additionally present in American society at this time is an interest in re-establishing connections with one's roots. This search for roots currently often takes the form of a geneological quest. It can also be seen, however, as a search for meaning and for the philosophical and theological roots which have traditionally enabled people to come to some understanding of who they are.

In the midst of these various societal and individual concerns is a growing interest in moral and ethical issues in various professions. Modern technology has complicated some traditional concerns--for example, questions around the right or obligation to prolong life and the methods of determining death when physiological functions are continued only by mechanical means. There is also increasing recognition of the many other aspects of modern medical practice in which moral decisions are being made, knowingly or unknowingly.[6]

Watergate disclosures, as well as other political and social problems related to the corruption of power and personal avarice, have challenged the law profession to examine its practices and ethical commitments. In the twentieth century even the military has been subjected to sharp ethical inquiry, particularly in the area of obedience to authority when inhumane acts are involved.

Within the past decade in the United States there has been a notable increase in courses in applied ethics at both undergraduate and graduate levels. The Hastings Center Study completed in 1980 estimates that 11,000-12,000 applied ethics courses are now being taught in colleges and universities.[7] In addition some professions, including social work, have either revised their ethical codes or have instituted new ones.

This trend toward increasing study of moral and ethical issues indicates the presence of a challenge to laissez faire attitudes in some parts of the academic world toward moral issues. This societal trend underlines the need in social work to attend to certain epistemological issues related to a predominantly positivistic definition of knowledge in which values are seen as preferences and the basis of ethical prescriptions is largely unanalyzed.

Footnotes

[1]T. Walter Wallbank and Allistair Taylor, Civilization - Past and Present, 2 vols. (Chicago: Scott, Foresman, 1942), 2:121-122.

[2]Gerald Holton, Thematic Origins of Scientific Thought, Kepler to Einstein (Cambridge, Massachusetts: Harvard University Press, 1973), pp. 454-455.

[3]J. Bronowski, The Ascent of Man (Boston: Little Brown, 1973), pp. 205-218.

[4]David Bohm, "On Insight and Its Significance, for Science, Education, and Values," Teachers College Record 80 (February 1979):411.

[5]Albert C. Outler, "Loss of the Sacred," Christianity Today 3, January 1981.

[6]See, for example, Tom L. Beauchamp and James F. Childress, _Principles of Biomedical Ethics_ (New York: Oxford University Press, 1979); Albert R. Jonsen et al., "The Ethics of Medicine: An Annotated Bibliography of Recent Literature," _Annals of Internal Medicine_ 92 (1980): 136-141; and various issues of the periodical, _The Hastings Center Report_.

[7]_The Teaching of Ethics in Higher Education_ (Hastings-on-Hudson, New York: The Hastings Center, 1980), p. 5.

CHAPTER V

THEORIZING IN SOCIAL WORK

History of Science in the Profession

Social work is embedded in the culture of its times.
It came into being in this period of rapid scientific
and technological development and is influenced by associated dominant modes of thinking. In addition, particularly because of its concern for people in trouble, it
has been profoundly influenced at various periods by the
social crises and upheavals which have taken place in
the last hundred years--wars and rumors of war, dislocations and abuses associated with industrial growth,
the need for labor of varying levels of skill, depres-
sions and grinding poverty, and the changing fabric of
social and family life. Since social work sees persons
as essentially social beings, its conceptualizing has
sometimes been caught in various tides, currents, and
whirlpools related to these human social phenomenon. A
word of caution is in order with reference to the discussion here. It is not possible in a few pages to do
justice to the many faceted approach which became social
work, even when confining the discussion to direct practice. There is always the danger of choosing selectively those aspects which support one's point of view.
While recognizing this potential pitfall, an effort will
be made to highlight the trends most significant for the
discussion here.

Social work can be seen as having arisen because of
the effects of industrialization on human life. Urban
population increased as did the evidences of poverty,
and the contrasts between the poor and the affluent became more visible. In addition, the maintenance of
human life became increasingly dependent upon the pro-
ducts of industry. The Charity Organization Societies
were a response to need in this kind of world. The earliest workers in the charity organization societies were
volunteers. However, there soon developed a place for
people who could devote themselves to these programs,
but who also were obliged to support themselves. This
gradual change from volunteer to employed staff had an
effect on a growing desire for a recognized profession
of social work.

In addition, leaders in the Charity Organization
Societies became increasingly concerned with the importance of more knowledge if people were to be truly helped. The recognition of the need to know more provided

33

a strong impetus for the development of a literature and the growth of training efforts. In 1898 the New York Charity Organization Society started a summer training program based upon the apprenticeship model. The recognized limitations of this type of training by itself led to the development in 1904 of a one year training program at the New York School of Philanthrophy which eventually became the Columbia University School of Social Work.

The recognized need for knowledge by those seeking ways to help people, the development of employed staff, and the expansion of training programs affiliated with the academic world led to a growing literature and increasingly organized efforts at conceptualizing practice. In addition, the interest in obtaining recognition as a profession developed early and contributed significantly to the effort to develop the knowledge base seen as a necessary requirement for professional status.

The struggle for professional recognition has suffered various vicissitudes over the years and an underlying insecurity about such status continues into the present, sometimes contributing to internecine struggles within social work itself. This underlying concern for professionalism at times becomes entangled in the issue of the relationship of social work to science. The roots of this problem can be found in some of the historical factors discussed here.

The place of science received some direct attention in various social work publications in the early part of this century. The word science, however, is used in a variety of ways. It sometimes seems to have meant primarily the effort to organize knowledge. Then as now the word itself served different purposes. One dictionary[1] gives the following among the first of many definitions of science: "The state or fact of knowing; knowledge or cognizance of something specified or implied," or "knowledge acquired by study; acquaintance with or mastery of any department of learning," or "trained skill." In the sense of these definitions, early interest in social work in becoming scientific can be seen to be basically an interest in organizing knowledge and ideas in ways which could be useful in understanding and improving the programs of the Societies.

In the Western world in this particular historical period, science was coming to have a more specific meaning. The Oxford dictionary also says of science, "in

modern use, often - Natural and Physical Science."
During the period in which social work was developing,
efforts were being made to apply the methods of the
physical sciences in many fields including the social
sciences.

In early social work literature it is not always
clear which definition of science was being used and
sometimes there is a rather confusing mixture. Gradually, however, social work, like the culture at large,
came to use the term science primarily in the more restricted sense. The scientific approach thus adopted
was based upon the idea of causality viewed somewhat
simplistically and mechanistically.[2] An early theme
in the charity organization societies was an effort to
identify the causes of poverty both in society and in
persons in need in this society. While modern social
work looks askance at some of these early efforts to
locate causes of poverty in individuals, what was important in this perspective was the optimistic view
rooted in faith in science that, once causes were identified, science would show how things could be changed
in a kind of linear cause and effect system.

Another aspect of this more restricted view of
science was the emphasis upon the scientific method defined as the use of objective observations based upon
sense data with emphasis upon the importance of replic-
able studies by other observers. This attitude came to
predominate in the social sciences, which were also developing during this period and is discussed later in
the chapter on positivism.

Early social workers had to rely on common sense
and native endowment which enabled them to be sympathetic
and responsive to the human need with which they were
confronted. Some early sources indicate an awareness
of the problem posed by the varying perceptions of different workers observing the same person.[3]

A number of these themes were drawn together by
Karpf who attempted a study of science and social work
using case records from family agencies, often the successors to the Charity Organization Societies. He emphasized the importance of "the social, psychological,
and biological sciences" to social work. He said:

> But even these limited data and the discussion
> based on them leave no room for doubt as to
> the necessity for scientific knowledge regard-
> ing all phases of human life with which the

social worker comes in contact. Over and over
again it became evident how inadequate and un-
reliable are the case worker's bases for her
judgments, opinions and efforts at controlling[4]
the behavior of her clients.

He continued:

Social work cannot hope to be as effective as
it might be unless it bases its techniques on
more adequate scientific data than is now the
case. Nor can it hope to acquire the status
and recognition due it as an important profession unless it accumulates a body of knowledge
and principles which will distinguish the professionally trained social worker from the untrained worker and from lay persons attempting
to attack the same problems. The professionally
trained social worker should be equipped with
the specialized knowledge and experience which
are the possession of the social work frater-
nity by virtue of its continuous search after
the truths regarding man and his social life,
developed by the different sciences and applicable to social work problems. He should not
be obliged to depend on his own life experience
to provide the knowledge which will give him
the sureness of touch and certainty of approach
necessary to a high type of professional practice.[5]

Evident in this quote is the need for more knowledge for practice and professional status reasons, and
the inclination to seek this knowledge in the sciences.
These ideas can be seen as signs of the developing relationship between social work and modern science.
Karpf's concerns and recommendations foreshadow some of
the current issues in social work which are addressed
here.

It was somewhat later when Gordon Hamilton indicated an expanded view of the potential of science to provide solutions for problems associated with differing
opinions within social work. She said:

I must also remind you that we can only have
(differing) schools of thought before conclusive scientific data are secured. As
knowledge advances in a given area, speculation diminishes.[6]

Thus did social work adopt the general cultural assessment of science and the scientific method as potentially providing answers to meet a wide variety of needs. In this climate it became increasingly difficult to recognize the limitations of science in addressing all areas of human life.

Borrowing from Other Disciplines

From its beginnings social work has needed knowledge from other professions. As the importance of conceptualizing practice became clearer, it was natural to look to existing professions for ideas as well as information. In recent times there has been criticism of direct practice as too much influenced by the medical model--and hence too much concerned with pathology and curative efforts based upon a medical model.[7] (The example of the study, diagnosis and treatment approach is often mentioned in this context.) The use of information and concepts from other disciplines, including medicine and the social sciences, is related to the need to define social work and specify its knowledge base.

As social work activities developed, there was increased interest in seeking recognition as a profession. Flexner's negative answer in his paper "Is Social Work a Profession?" seems to have been both a setback to aspirations and a spur to greater effort.[8] It is significant that Flexner's major work was a study in 1910, sponsored by the Carnegie Foundation, on medical education in the United States and Canada. Applying the same criteria used for that study he found social work lacking, particularly in the areas of personal responsibility, distinctive knowledge, and techniques which could be taught to others.[9]

During the early formative years social work in some form was practiced in a variety of settings--e.g., medical hospitals, children's agencies, courts, and psychiatric clinics and institutions. In medical and psychiatric settings workers performed a liaison function between medical staff and the patient, family, and community. While quite consistently emphasizing the social environment, both personal and physical, social work had difficulty defining a unique function and separating itself from the position of auxiliary to other more established professions, notably medicine and law.

In the public welfare field there were also other kinds of confusion such as the continued use of volunteer or untrained staff and later the participation of politicians in the administration of public welfare agencies.

It was, and is, difficult to enunciate what is unique about social work in relation to other professions particularly in view of the variety of settings in which it is practiced. A kind of broadly defined purpose, organizational problems related to both practice and education, plus a functional affiliation with medicine in certain settings, were certainly contributory to the complexities of the task of defining social work as a profession. It also made it difficult to establish clearly the relevance of material from other disciplines to social work practice.

Whatever residue in modern social work can be attributed to the early use of the medical model, the situation became even more complicated with reference to psychiatry. Most sources ascribe social work's early interest to the need for psychiatric services for returning veterans of World War I and to related experiences of dealing with the hardships and dislocations in families that resulted from the war. Concomitantly Freud's work was becoming known and attracted much interest. His ideas seemed to have explanatory power in relationship to the complex human problems increasingly the focus of social work efforts.

Psychoanalytic theory became a dominant influence in practice, an influence that continued for many years, at times leading social workers to view themselves as functioning very much as psychiatrists. In the last fifty to sixty years much has been written, taught, and done in this area. At times the social worker was treated as auxiliary to the psychiatrist who was clearly the head of the team; later some social workers saw their practice as very much akin to psychoanalysis. Although issues such as these occasionally arise in the present, there seems to be greater assurance on the part of social workers that the emphasis upon the social, i.e. persons interacting with other persons and in societal structures defines their purpose and provides a guide for evaluating the relevance of psychiatric and psychoanalytic theory to their practice.[10]

Intertwined in the relationship of social work to medicine and later to psychiatry has been the issue of science. Medicine has traditionally seen itself as a kind of scientific art--i.e., using information from the relevant sciences, and applying scientific techniques both in research and in treatment, while using the healer's art in practice with particular individuals. It's utilization of the medical model may have been one reason why social work also traditionally has seen itself as partly science and partly art.

Freud saw himself as a scientist. He began his medical work in research and only turned to practice because of his need to earn a living and support his family. One biographer says, "Freud's urge for investigation and his desire for scientific knowledge led him to favor lay analysis; the relief of suffering was part of the medical profession of healing, and was not Freud's main objective."[11] Freud spent much of his time analyzing himself and a succession of patients. He sought to understand and organize his materials in scientific fashion. Terminology was borrowed from the scientific world--for example, the use of the word object to represent significant people in the patient's life, and other terms such as the mechanisms of defence.

Psychoanalysis and other related forms of psychotherapy, however, tend to be something of an embarrassment from the standpoint of modern empirical science in which objective observation, sense data, and replicability are of such vital importance. For some schools the trend in teaching social work practice has been away from psychoanalytic content and toward theories which lend themselves more readily to empirical studies--such as behavioristic and task centered approaches, examples of which will be discussed next. Some schools have emphasized later developments in psychiatry which had their origins in Freud's work, but which have different, often broader, perspectives. The work of Otto Rank, Harry Stack Sullivan, Anna Freud, and Eric Erikson are illustrations.

It should be noted here that the narrow perspective of empirical science which is so influential in the United States is not shared by some of these theorists from a European background. In this country the view is common that the study of discrete behavior most nearly meets the criteria of science. For other theorists, such as Erikson, it is the whole person which is most important, and specifically human characteristics receive primary emphasis.

Falling clearly into the European philosophical perspective, Erikson and Piaget have been criticized by Anglo-American psychologists for a lack of experimental rigor. Such psychologists challenge the construction of elaborate theories on the basis of limited empirical findings that possibly are derived from biased samples. Despite these criticisms, it is questionable whether any North American or British psychologists have built a system that has as much explanatory utility as Erikson's or Piaget's.[12]

In the search for knowledge relevant to practice social workers turned to the social sciences which were also undergoing considerable development in the United States. There seemed to be a rather consistent expectation that the social sciences would provide useful information. As social work training became established in the colleges and universities, there was evidence of some differences of opinion and probably some conflict between the teachers of social science and those involved in direct practice--especially with reference to who should do the primary teaching.[13] At certain points in recent history this conflict has resurfaced--for example, the current importance placed on a doctoral degree for faculty in schools of social work with less emphasis on the necessity, or even the need, for practice experience.

The growth of doctoral education in social work seems to be contributing to a gulf between practitioners and academicians--accenting a kind of difference in viewpoint which, as indicated above, has been present in social work from its earliest days. Partisans of one side or the other of these debates usually use terms like intuition and practice wisdom versus scientific objectivity and empirical validity. What is important here is the point made by Gordon in a recent review of a book on social work research. He says:

> But an overriding concern is the everwidening gap between practitioners and researchers. This has been aided and abetted by the movement of the research base from agencies to universities, where social work doctoral training is strongly influenced by the academic social sciences. Often, the result is methodologically impeccable research that is unintelligible or irrelevant to practitioners.[14]

It is suggested here that this dichotomy has its origins in a limited definition of knowledge as only that which is scientific--a definition based upon the philosophy of positivism.

The social sciences were also undergoing considerable development and expansion during these years of
growth in social work. Although other social sciences
are also important for social work, the primary discussion here will be in terms of sociology and psychology as the disciplines having the most direct relevance to practice. Warwick says:

> From the 1930s through the 1950s the positivist
> mode of thought became ever more deeply entrench-
> ed in the disciplines of sociology and psycho-
> logy. A philosophical force lending powerful
> support to tendencies already present was the
> logical positivism first developed by the Vienna
> Circle. As members of this school began to take
> positions in American universities in the 1930s,
> they found many enthusiastic adherents, not only
> in philosophy departments, but in the social
> sciences. The impact was enormous, even among
> many social scientists who had never heard of
> the Vienna School.[15]

Warwick attributes the influence of the positivist
philosophies represented by the Vienna School to World
War II and the migration of philosophers of science
from the Continent to the United States. As a result of
this migration, combined with cultural trends in this
country, social scientists came to accept the position,
and insist upon it for their students, that the only
acceptable method was that of empirical science characterized by experiment, objective observation, measure-
ment, and value neutrality.

Most social work faculty, and probably all with
doctoral degrees, have been exposed to this emphasis
upon science defined in essentially positivistic terms.
It can even be said that this emphasis has been dogmatic
in much the same way that dogma has been promulgated by
the institutional church in certain historical periods--
i.e., brooking no difference of opinion. In this case,
differences of opinion have often been dismissed as
subjectivism or intellectually suspect in other ways.
In a recent book Perlman says:

> Especially in our present age, when science and
> fact and proof are held in topmost esteem, it
> is unfashionable, to say the least, for a pro-
> fessional person to assert the moving quality
> and therapeutic potency of something one can-
> not put one's finger on, which is not subject
> to precise description, itemization, quantifi-

41

cation, analysis, or even to verification by one or more of the five senses.[16]

What is of particular importance here is the way this positivist philosophy has become built into modern thinking in social work as well as in other academic areas. In order to understand how this point of view permeates professional discourse it is necessary to make a conscious effort to question these assumptions which have become integral parts of customary ways of thinking. Cassell discusses the way different disciplines view the world from their own particular perspective and the obstacles these points of view can present to efforts to do interdisciplinary research. He says:

> A person is defined, in part, by his conceptions, by the paradigmatic structure of values and beliefs about the world that relates each conception to the other. To ask of someone that he be prepared to call that conceptual structure into question is to ask that he be prepared to give up a piece of himself. People do not hold white-knuckle tight to their frames of reference out of pure reason but because to give up a frame of reference is extremely unsettling.[17]

Before discussing positivism more specifically, including its origins and limitations, it is useful to consider in greater detail how the associated emphasis in social work on establishing a scientific base has tended to narrow not only what may be considered to be knowledge, but also what is defined as effective practice.

Current Efforts to Establish a Scientific Base

One of the reasons for the emphasis upon scientific knowledge in social work is the assumption that a scientific approach is the only really reliable way of knowing. For example, Briar and Miller say:

> It is important to note that a commitment to the scientific method is a value premise of social work. There are many conceivable avenues toward the accumulation of knowledge and, in the span of mankind, the method of science is a relative latecomer to the roster of alternatives. Thus, one may argue that a precise knowledge of man and his universe can best be obtained through divine revelation,

42

or through the authority and tradition of
society, or through common sense and intuition.

The choice of which alternative is more reward-
ing is, in the final analysis, a value judgment,
although rational arguments can be presented
in support of the method of science as the most
productive and potent. Appeal to rational argument is, in itself, a partial commitment to
science as is the basic premise that knowledge
is valuable.[18]

Some crucial assumptions are apparent in this quotation.
First, it advocates the choice of the scientific approach which seems to be posited as in opposition to
other possible approaches to knowledge. Second, the
implication is that only the scientific approach is rational, with the additional implication that it is scientific knowledge which is valuable. In the concluding
paragraph of the chapter from which the above quotation
is taken the assumptions become more explicit.

To the extent that we adhere to the values in-
herent in the commitment to the method of science, and to the extent that we hold as an
overriding ethic the improvement of the quality
of our services, we must assume that man is
knowable and that the social work procedure
will become primarily scientific.[19]

Science is thus represented as a chosen value which will
then serve to provide guidance for the ethical purpose
of improving the quality of services. The result is an
amalgam of science and ethics and a blurring of the
distinctions which characterize the different disciplines.

This is the context in which the question of effectiveness arises in much current professional discourse.
It is not generally recognized that the definition of
effectiveness is crucial. Decisions about what is to be
considered to be effective implicitly involve what is
thought to be valuable and ethical. In most research an
effort is made to apply scientific methods to define
and quantify the results of specific techniques which
are then to be tested for effectiveness in terms of concrete, directly observable results. The published findings, frequently called outcome studies, have often been
negative.

A study of this research shows a wide variety of problems associated with the methodologies used. After a careful, detailed, and extensive inquiry into available examples of this research, Wood says, "Such research can give little information about whether practice is effective or how to make it more effective."[20] Despite the recognized limitations of these studies, noted by Wood and others, a critical attitude toward the effectiveness of social work practice continues to be expressed in the literature and the same studies are often used as illustrations.

Wood's point of view is that research and casework processes are basically the same and that social workers should treat each case as a research project, as an opportunity to test theory scientifically. Following a description of the casework process involving such factors as a definition of the problem and its causes, a plan for what can be done, and an evaluation of the results, she says, "This is precisely the scientific process--the process of research itself."[21] She concludes:

Recommendations drawn from this 'study of studies' are that practitioners must become more aware of the similarity between the practice process and the research process and must apply the thought and methodology of research to practice; . . . and that researchers must generate studies that focus on process as well as on outcome and that lead to prescriptions for practice.[22]

Some of the current difficulties in social work over the question of effectiveness could be mitigated by the kind of cooperation Wood recommends. In this discussion, however, disagreement is expressed regarding the statement that research and casework processes are the same. While there are certainly some similarities, social work research for the most part is based upon a positivist philosophy in which all that is to be considered meaningful is that which can be defined in terms of objectified sense data. Effectiveness then is defined in these terms. Social work practice, however, is seen here to be intrinsically involved with what it means to be a person, often in ways not encompassed by positivist definitions. An elaboration of this point of view and its implications constitute the second part of this book.

For the present it is important to illustrate additionally the ways the emphasis on effectiveness, sci-

entifically defined and tested, pervades the social
work literature. Some advocates of this approach have
gone beyond Briar and Miller's positing of the scientific approach as the most desirable alternative in knowledge building and Wood's equating of research and casework processes, and have actively advocated approaches
deemed to be scientific in opposition to what is seen
as traditional practice. Some authors have sought support for this approach in their reading of history.
Lukton says:

> When the precursor of the National Conference
> on Social Welfare (the National Conference of
> Charities and Corrections) was formed in 1879,
> it did so by detaching itself from the American
> Social Science Association. The formation of
> the organization reflected the commitment of
> its members to a practice orientation, in con-
> trast with the membership of its parent body
> who subscribed to the creation of a sound
> theoretical base and the development of the
> tools of research. (Underlining added.)[23]

In the same context she says:

> On the whole, practitioners have made few con-
> tributions to social work knowledge concerning
> the effectiveness of their practice. They
> have tended to ignore the results of outcome
> studies, continuing to employ methods that
> some research has shown to be questionable.[24]

As can be seen by these references, as well as
those which follow, there is a tendency in social work
discourse to address the matter of science in social
work as an adversary issue with reference to actual
practice. Sometimes the argument takes the form of
citing research which seems to substantiate doubts about
the personal qualifications and interests of those who
enter the profession.[25] The reasons for this attitude
are not clear. What is clear, however, is that the result is often a confrontation rather than a joined effort to discover useful knowledge wherever and in whatever discipline it might be found.

An example of these problems can be seen in a recent and much discussed book, Effective Casework Practice: An Eclectic Approach,[26] which also originated in
an academic setting. Fischer seeks to build a case for
practice amenable to scientific evaluation. He selects
four components for this practice which he refers to as:

"structuring the intervention process, behavior modification, cognitive procedures, and empathy, warmth, and genuineness: the core conditions." The first three components refer to techniques which Fischer believes meet the requirements of scientifically demonstrable, effective techniques. For the fourth component he draws upon some of the empirical studies in psychology in which major efforts have been made to define and explain the operation of these aspects of a therapeutic relationship.

The polemical tone characteristic of this book complicates discussion of its primary points. The emphasis is upon a recommended scientific, rational approach versus "traditional casework." Traditional casework is consistently denigrated by the use of words such as "complacent," "enamored," "infatuation," "guesswork," and "traditional mythology." The reader who sees value in the heritage to be found in the history of casework, and who wishes to claim this heritage, may well find it difficult to attend to the real issues when the discussion is presented in this manner. The point that is important here, however, is the emphasis upon developing a scientific technology for practice. This technology is designed to correct a perceived deficit in the field. Fischer says:

> However, while the recognition of the necessity for techniques has been present, the development of such techniques, as pointed out previously has lagged considerably, to the point where there are few if any definitive guidelines available in traditional approaches as to what techniques to apply, to what kinds of problems, with what kinds of clients, in what kinds of situations.[27]

There is an effort to design these techniques to accomplish objectives which are to be "clear, specific, observable, and measurable."[28] The focus is therefore upon techniques for the purpose of changing behavior which can be observed. Fischer advocates what he calls an ecclectic approach whereby a technique or method is chosen because it is "effective" and he takes the position that this approach is atheoretical. He recommends a commitment "to the basic values of our responsibility to effectively help the people we serve,"[29] and expresses the belief that theories, particularly those of "traditional casework," are constraining and interfere with effectiveness.

The problem, however, is the definition of terms like effectiveness and helping. Definitions of what is to count as effectiveness and what helping means reflect philosophical as well as theoretical assumptions. The apparent simplicity of defining effective in terms of reports of changed behavior can be misleading. Perhaps one of the clearest examples of the limitations of this kind of definition can be seen in the occasional suicide which occurs just at the time a patient's behavior and demeanor seem to indicate recovery from a severe depression.

Fischer's effort to be ecclectic and atheoretical is very dependent upon behavioral theory and behavior modification methods. It also reflects the philosophy of positivism. The important point noted earlier and recurring throughout the discussion here is that made by Barrett:

> Every technique is put to use for some end, and this end is decided in the light of some philosophic outlook or other. The technique cannot produce the philosophy that directs it.[30]

It is not clear how Fischer would integrate the material discussed in his chapter on empathy, warmth and genuineness with the controlled use of techniques advocated in the earlier chapters. He sees no inconsistency, but there are problems which have not been addressed. He says:

> Now the point is not that there is anything wrong with the basic notion of 'relationship.' Rather, it is that vagueness, imprecision, and a lack of empirical evidence about its effects have plagued much of casework writing about relationship. Thus, to save--and to have a sound rationale for saving--the concept of relationship for practice, somewhat more rigor and certainly more precision about its meaning needs to be developed.[31]

The difficulty with this effort to introduce rigor and precision into the concept of relationship is that it risks narrowing the concept to the language of empirical science, particularly in emphasizing observable physical aspects. Such a limited framework fails to encompass all that is meaningful in human relationships and therefore does not address all that is relevant to social work practice. Fischer's interpretations illus-

trate some of the limitations associated with this perspective.

His discussion of the core conditions of relationship (empathy, warmth, and genuineness) makes extensive
use of the research in psychology on these factors in
the therapeutic relationship based primarily upon the
Truax and Carkhuff studies originating in Carl R. Roger's
work.[32] Fischer expresses the conviction that these
conditions are valuable because psychological research
shows that they contribute to positive outcomes in
treatment. Some of this research suggests, as he indicates, that the positive contribution of these aspects
of relationship occur in the work of therapists with
different theoretical orientations.

Instead of seeing this research evidence as confirmation of the importance of the concept of relationship in
social work practice, and as potentially helpful in
clarifying some of what practitioners mean by relationship, Fischer interprets the research as critical of
those he calls traditional caseworkers. At this point
his discussion moves from an emphasis upon empirical
studies to an argument for good, i.e., effective, versus
bad, i.e., traditional, caseworkers. He says:

It appears that, in marked contrast to traditional casework recommendations regarding what caseworkers should be like, the effective caseworker
has many different characteristics: deeply involved, deeply personal, deeply caring.[33]

The failure to recognize that the discussion has
moved to a different level is further illustrated by the
following sentence:

These effective people are uncommitted to rigid
dogmas and ideologies other than those which produce growth for themselves and others.[34]

Philosophical issues related to what is good, valuable,
and ethical are apparent here. When these issues are
not addressed directly, there is a tendency for them to
appear in the form of unexamined assumptions.

It has been noted that throughout his discussion of
various techniques Fischer relies on much of the research in behavior modification. What has become known
generally as the behavior modification approach is based
upon B. F. Skinner's work, first with animals and later
extrapolated to human subjects. Earlier related efforts

included Pavlov's experiments with conditioned reflexes in dogs and later Watson's work. The following description of Watson's work is relevant in this context.

In the second decade of this century John B. Watson (1925) gave birth to Behaviorism as the culmination of psychology's struggle to free itself from its roots in religious philosophy. His approach was objective and parsimonius, defining variables in terms of rigorous laboratory operations and theorizing close to the data. He redefined the subject matter of psychology in peripheral terms and provided a model of experimental objectivity that dominated American psychology during the first half of the century.[35]

B. F. Skinner and others following him have developed many techniques which are included under the general rubric of behavior modification. Researchers and clinicians have used the basic concepts in various ways.[36] Some, like Fischer, have tried to introduce a mix utilizing other theories such as the Truax and Carkhuff work in the qualities characterizing therapeutic relationships.

The criticism of behavior modification most frequently expressed is that it is essentially manipulative, as it is designed to use specific techniques, positive and negative, to change behavior in the desired direction. In the strictest forms of application of these techniques manipulation can be easily demonstrated, but if the desired behavioral results are achieved, philosophical questions related to manipulation are not considered relevant by its advocates. Some practices such as those associated with adversive conditioning in institutions have in fact raised ethical and legal questions resulting in some major court decisions.[37]

The advocates of behavioral modification techniques who utilize a variety of other concepts, including those pertaining to relationship, and who adhere to certain ethical principles regarding patient or client consent, do not believe their approach to be essentially manipulative.[38] To some degree their position is supported by the fact that very similar techniques have always been part of the way children are socialized by their parents and other caring people. (The word caring is perhaps crucial and suggests an additional dimension not required by behaviorism per se.)

A basic problem in the therapeutic use of behavior

modification can be seen to be the risk of error associated with oversimplification. Language often plays a part in this kind of error which may result from the reduction of behavior to scientific terms not designed to describe the intricate processes characteristic of the human mind.[39]

Another problem associated with behavior modification, as with various other theories, is the expansion of the concepts into situations far beyond the original limited experimental data. The most notable example of this is the influence of Skinner's idea of a Utopia based upon these approaches described in Walden Two. The application of behavioral techniques to societal problems, Skinner believes, would obviate the need for political action or even for "wisdom and common sense." Of the problems of overconsumption, pollution, and threats of atomic warfare Skinner says:

> The choice is clear: either we do nothing and allow a miserable and probably catastrophic future to overtake us, or we use our knowledge about human behavior to create a social environment in which we shall live productive and creative lives, and do so without jeopardizing the chances that those who follow us will be able to do the same. Something like Walden Two would not be a bad start.[40]

There seems to be a human tendency to develop great expectations for theories born in humbler circumstances. In the context of the modern world it would appear almost inevitable that this expansionist temptation would exploit the materials and vocabulary of science. Erikson speaking of Piaget and himself calls attention to this issue:

> Most of us have our roots in one or the other, in the experimental or the clinical methods: that is, we know man either when he is well enough to lend parts of himself for study in suitable settings, or sick enough to fall apart into discernible fragments of behavior. The workers who turn to the first, the experimental method, are on the whole cautious in making any promises regarding their ability to reveal man's nature. But it is clear that their methodological modesty disguises the expectation that all their reliable data added together will eventually be equal to the total functioning of man-- if, indeed, man could only be prevailed upon to

realize that life would be much more manageable
if he would consent to be the sum of his reli-
ably investigated parts. I belong to another
breed, the clinicians, who are modest and vain
in different ways. Much less cautious, we speak
with relative ease of the core of man's person-
ality and of stages in its development. But
then, our subjects want to become whole; and
the clinician must have some theories and methods which offer the patient a whole world to be
whole in. Mistaking our patients gratitude for
verification, we are sometimes sure that we
could explain or even guide mankind if it would
only consent to be our collective patient.[41]

Before leaving the subject of the relationship of
cultural emphasis on science to contemporary theorizing
in social work, note should be taken of two other examples of efforts to incorporate scientific techniques
into practice. The first to be considered here is the
task centered approach developed by Reid and Epstein at
the University of Chicago.

The task centered approach has evolved over a period
of several years. The emphasis is upon planned, short
term intervention whereby the social worker together with
the client decides on a specific focus for treatment efforts. Primary emphasis is placed on specificity based
upon what the client requests, wants or needs. The
social worker has the responsibility of helping the
client decide upon a task which reasonably can be accomplished and then assisting in finding ways to accomplish
it. The approach was designed to allow for testing
through empirical research and various studies have been
undertaken.

The task centered approach utilizes behavioral modification techniques but recognizes their limitations in
dealing with some human problems. Reid says:

The concept of task provides a way of integrating a technology for behavior change, on
the one hand, with strategies for effecting
other kinds of action often required to resolve problems faced by social work clients.[42]

He concludes:

Fundamentally our interest is not behavioral
methods as such but in methods that are scientifically testable.[43]

The task centered approach would seem to be potentially helpful in many situations with which social workers are confronted. It can correct for some of the problems which arise when problems are viewed so globally that efforts become diffuse. This can be the result in situations where the client's problems are in fact global and overwhelming and there is need to partialize if anything constructive is to be done.

Difficulties are introduced, however, by a too rigorous effort to fit the model to the requirements of a scientific experiment. In the major study of effectiveness reported[44] a number of limitations are introduced to establish such empirical conditions.

The study is designed to test the effects of the task centered approach against the effects of what Reid calls supportive attention, which is referred to as a placebo treatment. The effort is to try to isolate variables, but the result is a semantic confusion in relationship to the concept of supportive treatment which has long been a part of casework practice. A placebo in a medical context is an inert substance which may be reported as effective because of various psychomatic factors connected with receiving anything at all.[45] It is suggested here that an error is introduced by equating a human, person to person activity with the administration of an inert substance.

In addition there are other questions raised by the use of a supportive attention approach as a control. Supportive attention as defined for this study was not designed to deal with the complex factors generally recognized as involved in supportive treatment in social work practice. The following is the description given:

> Practitioners were given various options in conducting supportive sessions. They could let the client discuss immediate concerns, explore historical material, obtain further information about the clients' problems or social situation, or, with children, engage in play activities. They were not, however, to develop tasks, use any of the task-centered activities, employ such change-oriented techniques as advice giving or providing explanations of the client's behavior, or to take any actions in the client's social system aimed at alleviating his problem.[46]

It is notable that the practitioners used for this experiment were first year casework students. Speaking at a meeting following the publication of this study Reid indicated that there had been difficulties in using experienced practitioners in tests of this kind. He declined at that time to elaborate on the problems. It is unfortunate that these issues have not been dealt with directly. The failure to do so leaves the interpretation to the readers. Given the present problems in communication between academic researchers and social work practitioners, there is a risk that this type of study will be used to criticize practice as though it were in fact a study of task centered versus supportive treatment, i.e., something often called traditional casework.

Supportive treatment in practice is a specific effort to support strengths in clients in their efforts to deal with their problems. The social worker may use a variety of approaches to a particular client. Changes which result from these efforts are often attributed to the relationship between client and worker. It is important to recognize that it is difficult to assess effectiveness, as it is usually defined, in this context as most supportive treatment situations do not meet the requirements of empirical research. An oversimplification of the social work process in an effort to meet empirical standards can introduce additional errors, such as failing to recognize what is operative but has not been acknowledged. In addition, the difficulty in assessing the degree to which the results of such research studies can be generalized has rarely been recognized in the literature. The effect is often to polarize practitioners and researchers to the detriment of the work of both.

One other area in which efforts to make social work more scientific impinge on practice can be seen is in the application of general systems theory to the field. Systems theories developed within the context of the sciences and arose as a result of the recognition of the limitations of earlier mechanical, linear cause and effect theories. The emphasis is upon the interaction within systems at various levels and the interplay between, or among, the systems. Various terms have been applied to social work such as macro, mezzo, and micro to apply to the larger society, the community and various organizations, and the personal level of individuals and families. At the present time an emphasis on ecosystems is receiving much attention. The ecosystem emphasizes the interaction between persons and various aspects of their environment. Attributing some of the current difficulties in practice to the older mechanistic model of sci-

53

ence,[47] Germain advocates an ecosystems approach as an overall orientation for social work theory and practice.

Systems concepts can help to clarify some of the complexities of the interactions between humans and their physical and social environments. Sometimes a new way of describing a phenomenon previously recognized but in different terms can be enlightening. Difficulties arise with a systems approach, as with other theories, when an effort is made to present it as the solution to all the problems of conceptualization in practice.

There have been, and continue to be, problems in applying scientific techniques to social work practice, illustrated by the efforts to demonstrate effectiveness. There is, however, a continuing need, shared by both practitioners and researchers, to define and evaluate appropriate and helpful practices. Scientific technology can be useful in this effort, but such technology should be integrated into a philosophical approach adequate to the subject matter.

In referring to this problem in medicine, Norman Cousins says:

> The basic issue is not the usefulness of the new technology. It is the philosophical frame in which the new technology is brought into play and how it is used.[48]

Later in the same chapter he says of his hospital experience:

> And there was the utter void created by the longing--ineradicable, unremitting, pervasive--for warmth of human contact. A warm smile and an outstretched hand were valued even above the offerings of modern science, but the latter were far more accessible than the former.

> I became convinced that nothing a hospital could provide in the way of technological marvels was as helpful as an atmosphere of compassion.[49]

Social work has traditionally been concerned with these additional dimensions of human life, and there is some public recognition of this role of social workers in society.[50] These concerns are intrinsically involved with moral issues. Moral and ethical questions

however, represent an area of inquiry which cannot be
understood in only scientific terms and which in the
light of the discussion here can be seen to pose a dilemma for modern social work.

Attitudes Toward Moral and Ethical Issues

As indicated earlier there is a tendency within
social work to accept the perspective associated with
the philosophy of positivism in which values are seen
to be merely preferences and knowledge is seen to be
that which is scientific.

For example, Gordon says:

In their basic meaning, value and knowledge
are quite distinct and run on quite indepen-
dent meaning tracks.

.   .   .

Knowledge, on the other hand, denotes the
picture man has built up of the world and
himself as it is, not as he might wish or
fantasy or prefer it to be. It is a picture derived from the most rigorous interpretation he is capable of giving to the
most objective sense data he is able to ob-
tain. An assertion of how things are that
is found to hold when confronted with objective data rigorously interpreted is
central to the idea of knowledge. Thus
knowledge refers to what, in fact, seems
to be, established by the highest standards
of objectivity and rationality of which man
is capable. Value refers to what man pre-
fers or would want to be with a degree of
attachment that may involve all the loyalty
or devotion or sacrifice of which he is
capable.[51]

Social work has always been concerned with values
and this concern became more explicit as the development toward professionalism grew. Early studies of
social work all emphasized the commitment to values as
well as the necessity of building knowledge.[52] The
National Association of Social Workers (NASW) established the first official code of ethics in 1960, revised
it in 1967, and recently passed a totally rewritten code
which was implemented starting in 1980. The latest code
has the dual purpose of serving as a guide for practice
and as a basis for adjudication in the case of complaints.

There have also been two recent efforts on the part of the NASW to define a conceptual framework for social work practice. The report of the most recent effort includes a statement emphasizing social work's concern with the quality of life and including the assertion that:

> Transactions between individuals and others in their environment should enhance the dignity, individuality and self-determination of everyone. People should be treated humanely and with justice.[53]

There does not seem to be much recognition in the profession that this interest in, and commitment to, values and ethical concerns has relevance to a discussion of knowledge in social work and that it contains an implicit challenge to the predominant positivist definition of knowledge. Some writers have alluded to the issue. Vigilante is one of the few who has addressed it directly. He believes that the emphasis upon science as defined by the logical positivists, which social work has adopted from the culture and specifically from the social sciences, has contributed to the rise of individualism and the undermining of community values and organizations which represent those values. He says:

> Social workers have religiously clung to values over the seventy years of the development of the profession and have not done these values justice. We seem to cling to them intuitively, out of faith, as a symbol of our humanitarianism. We have not treated them with the seriousness befitting their role as the fulcrum of practice.[54]

He sees the problem for social work as located in the continuing tendency to interpret the definition of science in strict conformity with logical positivism in which values are considered to be personal preferences with little intellectual standing.

The lack of integration between these emphases in social work on knowledge as basically scientific and values as preferences, has not received much attention and results in unacknowledged inconsistencies. For example, Fischer suggests that values do not need to be justified (apparently also doubting that justification is possible) but continues "at the very least their implementation must be justified because this involves expense, financial and personal, and affects many

56

people.[55] In addition, Briar and Miller refer to the
way the fundamental principle of the intrinsic value of
the individual person in social work has roots in the
Judeo-Christian tradition and humanistic emphases in
this country. In addition to Genesis and the United
States Constitution, they refer to Walt Whitman. They
call this concern with the value of the individual a
"troublesome principle" and say:

> Its validity as truth has been questioned
> through the ages; the existential nihilism
> of a Camus or a Sartre was anticipated five
> thousand years earlier by Job.[56]

At the end of this chapter on values in casework the
authors discuss the way the work of the social worker
is differentiated from others. They say that the worker:

> Does not indoctrinate an ideology--at least
> not a political or theological ideology--and
> hence is radically different from the brain
> washer or priest--who may also effect cures
> in their clients. (Underlining added.)[57]

The tendency to equate dogmatism with religion, as
indicated earlier, can be seen to be rooted in the history of science. The development of logical positivism
is intertwined with this history. Academic social work,
where much of the current literature originates, is
still very committed to the positivistic definition of
science. In addition, however, both academic social
workers and practitioners are expected to subscribe to
certain values and ethical commitments. Sometimes, as
indicated in the earlier discussion, an uneasy integration is accomplished by blurring distinctions associated with the different disciplines. The lack of fit,
however, between these two commitments (i.e., to positivist science and to ethical convictions) does not receive much attention and as a result hidden assumptions,
such as that all religion is dogmatic and ideological,
continue to operate, even while recognition is given to
the roots of these values in religious and moral tradition.

Moral choices and ethical commitments in social
work activities in a highly technological industrial
society are too complicated and important to be left to
operate in this unexamined way. It almost seems as if
social work has sought to hold onto values which have
been severed from their roots. The reason these values

have not been seriously challenged within the profession is probably because individual social workers have either remained connected to these roots in a personal way[58] and/or have been able to compartmentalize intellectually so that values and the search for scientific knowledge are not seen to be integrally related.

Although so far this dichotomy has rarely been challenged directly, there is an underlying uneasiness that leaves the profession vulnerable to external pressures from cultural influences and internal stresses. It is worth considering the possibility that internecine struggles, which seem to pit the empiricists in the profession against the practitioners, represent a kind of covert effort to deal with this problem--and to resolve it in favor of empirical science. It is the purpose of the discussion here to open up these epistemological issues to direct discussion and consideration with the expectation that the result for social work will be integrative rather than divisive.

In Part Two aspects of these issues are examined in greater depth, beginning with a discussion of the history of positivism and its relationship to the philosophy of science.

Footnotes

[1] The Oxford Universal Dictionary, s.v. "Science."

[2] See Carel Germain, "Casework and Science: A Historical Encounter," in Theories of Social Casework, eds. Robert W. Roberts and Robert H. Nee (Chicago: University of Chicago Press, 1970), pp. 5-32.

[3] See, for example, Ada E. Sheffield, Case Study Possibilities, 1922, quoted in Maurice J. Karpf, The Scientific Basis of Social Work (New York: Columbia University Press, 1931), p. 39.

[4] The emphasis on control has a complex history and role in social work. See, for example, Joel F. Handler, The Coercive Social Worker (Chicago: Rand McNally College Publishing, 1973). At the present time the issue of control can be found in somewhat different form in approaches designed to meet the requirements of empirical research. See the following discussion of the work of Fischer and Reid.

[5]Karpf, The Scientific Basis of Social Work, p. 364.

[6]Gordon Hamilton, "The Underlying Philosophy of Social Case Work," The Family XXII (July 1941):140.

[7]See, for example, discussion in Lydia Rapoport, "Crisis Intervention as a Mode of Brief Treatment," in Theories of Social Casework, eds. Roberts and Nee, pp. 275-276.

[8]Abraham Flexner, "Is Social Work a Profession?" Proceedings of the 42nd National Conference of Charities and Corrections, Maryland, 1915.

[9]Encyclopedia of Social Work, s.v. "Flexner, Abraham," p. 485.

[10]See "Conceptual Frameworks II," Social Work 26 (January 1981).

[11]Paul Roazen, Freud and His Followers (New York: Alfred A. Knopf, 1971), p. 134.

[12]Kathleen M. White and Joseph C. Speisman, Adolescence (Monterey, California: Brooks/Cole, 1977), p. 12.

[13]Karpf, The Scientific Basis of Social Work, pp. 375-380.

[14]William Gordon, "Does Social Work Research Have a Future? A Book Review," Social Work Research and Abstracts 16 (Summer 1980):3.

[15]Warwick, The Teaching of Ethics in the Social Sciences, p. 27.

[16]Helen Harris Perlman, Relationship, The Heart of Helping People (Chicago: University of Chicago Press 1979), p. 22.

[17]Eric J. Cassell, "How Does Interdisciplinary Work?," in Knowledge, Value and Belief, eds. H. Tristram Engelhardt, Jr. and Daniel Callahan (Hastings-on-Hudson, New York: The Hastings Center, 1977), p. 357.

[18]Scott Briar and Henry Miller, Problems and Issues in Social Casework. (N.Y.: Columbia University Press, 1971), p. 79.

[19]Ibid., p. 88.

[20]Katherine M. Wood, "Casework Effectiveness: A New Look at the Research Evidence," Social Work 23 (November 1978):451.

[21]Ibid., p. 446.

[22]Ibid., p. 456.

[23]Rosemary Creed Lukton, "Barriers and Pathways to Integrating Research and Practice in Social Work: Suggestions for Innovation in the MSW Curriculum," Journal of Education for Social Work 16 (Spring 1980):20.

[24]Ibid.

[25]See, for example, Richard L. Simpson, "Understanding the Utilization of Research in Social Work and Other Allied Professions," in Sourcebook on Research Utilization, eds. Allen Rubin and Aaron Rosenberg (New York: Council on Social Work Education, 1979), p. 23 and footnotes.

[26]Joel Fischer, Effective Casework: An Eclectic Approach (New York: McGraw-Hill, 1978).

[27]Ibid., p. 61.

[28]Ibid., p. 44.

[29]Ibid., p. 68.

[30]Barrett, The Illusion of Techniques, p. 105.

[31]Fischer, p. 190.

[32]Charles B. Truax and Robert R. Carkhuff, _Toward Effective Counseling and Psychotherapy: Training and Practice_ (Chicago: Aldine, 1967).

[33]Fischer, p. 213.

[34]_Ibid._, pp. 213-214.

[35]John N. Marquis, "Behavior Modification Theory: B. F. Skinner and Others," in _Operational Theories of Personality_, ed. Arthur Burton (New York: Brunner/ Mazel, 1974), p. 351.

[36]_Encyclopedia of Social Work_, 17th Ed., s.v. "Social Casework and Social Group Work: The Behavioral Modification Approach," by Edwin J. Thomas.

[37]See, for example, _Clonce_ v. _Richardson_, 379 F. Supp. 338 (W.D.Mo. 1974); and _Knecht_ v. _Gilman_, 448 F. 2d. 1136 (8th Cir. 1973), in Reed Martin, _Legal Challenges to Behavior Modification_. (Champaign, Illinois: Research Press, 1975), pp. 169, 172-173.

[38]See, for example, Arthur Schwartz and Israel Goldiamond, _Social Casework, A Behavioral Approach_, New York: Columbia University Press, 1975, pp. 271-273.

[39]See, for example, John Flynn, "Behavior Modification: Communication and Psychological Manipulation," _Soundings_, V. LX, No. 1, (Spring 1977).

[40]B. F. Skinner, _Walden Two_, 2nd ed. with a new introduction by the author (New York: MacMillan, 1976), p. xvi.

[41]Erik H. Erikson, _Insight and Responsibility_, (New York: W. W. Norton, 1964), p. 136.

[42]William J. Reid, _The Task-Centered System_ (New York: Columbia University Press, 1978), p. 106.

[43]_Ibid._, p. 107.

[44]Ibid., pp. 225-329.

[45]The complexity of the issue of placebos in medicine, including ethical considerations related to deception, is discussed in Norman Cousins, Anatomy of an
Illness as Perceived by the Patient (New York: W. W.
Norton, 1979; Bantam Books, 1981), pp. 49-69.

[46]Reid, p. 234.

[47]Carel Germain, "Casework and Science: A Historical Encounter," in Robert W. Roberts and Robert H. Nee,
eds., Theories of Social Casework (Chicago: University
of Chicago Press, 1970), pp. 3-32; and Carel Germain,
"Social Casework," in Harleigh B. Trecker, ed., Goals
for Social Welfare, 1973-1993 (New York: Association
Press, 1973), pp. 125-137.

[48]Cousins, Anatomy of an Illness, p. 138.

[49]Ibid., p. 154.

[50]C. David Condie et al., "How the Public Views
Social Work," Social Work 23 (January 1978):47-53.

[51]William Gordon, "Knowledge and Value: Their Distinction and Relationship in Clarifying Social Work
Practice," Social Work 10 (July 1965):32-39.

[52]See summaries in Donald Brieland, "Historical
Overview," Social Work 22 (September 1977):341-352.

[53]"Working Statement on the Purpose of Social Work,"
Social Work 26 (January 1981):6.

[54]Joseph Vigilante, "Between Values and Science:
Education for the Profession During a Moral Crisis or
Is Proof Truth?" Journal of Education for Social Work
10 (Fall 1974):114.

[55]Fischer, p. 10.

[56]Briar and Miller, p. 33.

[57]<u>Ibid</u>., p. 52.

[58]See Tokayer, "What Social Work Practitioners Conceive as Social Work Philosophy in the Nature of Their Practice."

PART TWO

WIDENING THE PHILOSOPHICAL BASE

OF KNOWING IN SOCIAL WORK

CHAPTER VI

POSITIVISM AND THE PHILOSOPHY OF SCIENCE

It has been suggested at various points so far in this discussion that positivism is a pervasive philosophical influence in social work. This influence can be seen to be operative in a number of different ways. Academic programs, particularly at the doctoral level, exert pressure on social work activities where these programs impinge on practice--directly in the training of social work students and less directly but nevertheless pervasively in much of the literature describing and evaluating practice.

In a broader sense, positivism can be seen to be influential in the ways social work and social workers share in cultural attitudes in general, especially in the cultural evaluation of science seen from a positivist point of view. There is then a certain kind of fit between the criticisms originating in this point of view and directed against practitioners from academic sources, and the internal attitudes of the practitioners who, due to academic training and acculturation, in some measure accept this criticism.

While there is occasional discomfort and protest that this perspective does not do justice to the human endeavor in which they are engaged, practitioners in general have not been aware of the philosophical origin of these pressures and the limited perspective which they represent. As a result they for the most part have not identified the philosophical source of their discomfort. The adversary way in which the issues have often been discussed in the literature contributes to this difficulty so that anger appears to be defensiveness in the face of justified criticism, and attention is diverted from what has been left out of this positivistic perspective.

It is important that the real issues be identified and that the level of discourse be broad enough to encompass these issues. The effort here will be to discuss the development of the philosophy of positivism so that its historical origins are apparent and its limitations for the human activity that is social work can become clearer.

Positivism is commonly used to refer to the philosophical position in which knowledge is defined as scientific fact, ascertained by sense experience, and utilizing techniques associated with mathematical logic. One reviewer refers to Fischer's position as one of logical positivism which involves the "denial of the validity of any knowledge that is not based on controlled empirical observation."[1] Empirical is another term frequently used in social work discourse usually with reference to objective observations in science. In philosophy, empiricism may refer more broadly to experience, albeit in modern usage, particularly in positivism, this usually means sense experience.

The apparent simplicity in conventional definitions of positivism, and related terms, in modern culture is misleading. There are a number of important philosophical strands, utilizing variations of these terms, which need to be recognized for their historical contributions as well as their continuing influence.

Much of the philosophical thought which is relevant to the discussion here is related to struggles with the Cartesian dualism mentioned earlier. In academic social work there seems to be a general acceptance of the idea that the real world is objective and out there and that it is known by way of methods found useful in physics. These methods are usually expected to be based upon sense data and mathematical techniques.

These basic ideas can be traced back to Descartes (1596-1650), whose thought took place in the context of the culture and knowledge of the seventeenth century. Starting with the I, in the Cogito Descartes had to find a way out of the extreme subjectivism of this position.

As indicated in the earlier discussion, theological ideas played an important part in Descartes' thought. He reasoned from a belief in a veracious God, who not only created the world but was also the quarantor of the truth of those aspects of the world which Descartes believed he could know clearly and distinctly. Knowing clearly and distinctly, however, involved the use of the sense organs and this presented a problem, since sense experiences are internal and may be illusory.

Descartes, reasoning in the light of the physiology and neurology of his day, was able to objectify the body and the separate sense organs which as part of the objective world were also stimulated by it. However, what then became known to mind through this stimulation was an inner subjective experience. Descartes, a man of many talents, was also a mathematician and scientist.

He concluded that that part of experience received from the senses which could be dealt with through mathematical techniques could be considered part of the external, material world about which God would not allow him to be deceived.

This sundering of sense experience into two parts (that which can be considered part of the external world because it can be converted into meter readings, or something comparable, and that which is personal, private and subjective) is present, but not clearly recognized in most efforts to define knowledge in social work and to make it scientific.[2] Implications of this dichotomy for social work practice will be discussed later with reference to the objective-subjective problem in the chapter on knowledge of the person. The present discussion will continue to trace the historical development of positivism.

Building on Descartes' ideas the British empiricist[3] Locke (1632-1704) developed the concept of primary and secondary qualities. Primary qualities were those dealt with by mathematical physics, i.e., shapes, mass, motion, and singleness or plurality, which were believed to be the true characteristics of the external world. All other data of the senses represented merely secondary qualities--those which existed only internally.

Locke promulgated the well known theory of the tabula rasa--the mind as a blank slate at birth developed through information received from sense experiences. Although there is overwhelming evidence of the inaccuracy of this view--in modern assessments of the condition of the fetus and the newborn infant and in Piaget's work, to cite but two examples--certain elements of this point of view seem to persist in behaviorism which is in a way the psychological paradigm for positivism. In approaches based upon behavior modification theory, observable behavior, which is all that counts, is manipulable by means of positive or negative outside pressures. It is almost as though Locke's blank slate had instead become a kind of switchboard for receiving outside stmuli and stimulating reactive behavior.

Hume (1711-1776), another of the British empiricists, moved philosophical thought further along the line leading to the modern positivists. According to Hume all truths were either matters pertaining to the relations of ideas, such as in logic or mathematics, or matters of fact, which he sought to ground in experi-

ences of the senses called impressions, which in more
recent times are referred to as sense data.[4] At one
point Hume commented that all books containing any
other kinds of statements should be burned--thus providing a useful quote for those who followed.[5]

It was Comte (1798-1857), the French philosopher,
who labelled his philosophy positivism--with reference
to the effort to distinguish the "positive" truths of
facts from what he saw as the speculations and unsub-
stantiated assumptions of the metaphysicians. Historically, Comte was not as influential as Hume, but the
use of the term positivism continues into the present.
Comte developed his idea of positivism as a kind of
historical coming of age of science following periods
dominated first by religion (with emphasis upon super-
stition and unfounded dogma) and then by metaphysics
(as abstract, meaningless speculation). While the concept of such discrete historical periods has not had
much acceptance, the basic attitudes toward theology
and metaphysics are similar to those reflected in modern positivism.

The term logical positivism is historically associated with the group of philosophers who came to be
known as the Vienna Circle (1924-1936)--most notably
Moritz Schlick, Rudolph Carnap, and Otto Neurath, whose
influence became dominant in the social sciences in the
United States. This group built on the work of Russell
and Whitehead in the Principia Mathematica, published
in 1910-13, dealing with logic and the foundations of
mathematics. Russell also utilized the work of the
physicist Mach (1838-1916) who sought to ground physics
in sensory experience. According to Barrett one sentence of Russell's summarizes the positivist position:

> Whatever knowledge is attainable, must be
> attained by scientific methods; and what sci-
> ence cannot discover, mankind cannot know.[6]

In his early writings Wittgenstein (1889-1951) developed in detail a view known as logical atomism.
Historically this thought bears a relationship to another Humean idea--that is, that observations of events
occurring sequentially cannot necessarily be said to
occur causally.[7] Mach and Helmholtz applied this to
their science, and thus established it in the thought of
the empiricists.

The notion of cause or force as an occult power
or inner bond between phenomena was to be ban-

ished from the physical sciences. Science
states only the co-presence and co-variation
of facts within the world.[8]

Logical atomism combined this idea with techniques of
mathematical logic which were then shown to be tautologies. "Any one fact can either be the case or not be
the case, and everything else remains the same."[9] The
result of this line of thought was to suggest a world
of discrete entities where nothing was of necessity
related to anything else. Wittgenstein himself did not
rest with this philosophical approach and in his later
thought developed a theme of mysticism which was only
hinted at in his earlier writing. What is important in
the discussion here is the way some of these earlier
ideas are still operative in modern positivism.

For the positivists the truths of philosophy became positive truths which were matters of fact or
logical truths which were tautologies. Matters of fact
were to be found by scientific methods involving the
techniques of mathematical physics, which is the paradigm for all science for the positivists, and which was
the apparent embodiment of the part of sense data which
for Descartes could be considered to be part of the objective world. The role of philosophy was to describe
the formal logical structures in the reasoning of the
scientists, including the selection of the various sym-
bols of mathematics and language. Only the form of the
logic was to be considered relevant and philosophers
were no longer to be involved with traditional concerns
about the content of reasoning about the world--only
with these methods. Later much philosophical thought
consisted of efforts to elaborate some of these ideas
extending into the areas of linguistics and semantics
as well as mathematical logic. What became known as
analytic philosophy was much involved with positivistic
thinking in its early development.

There were of course other major philosophers during this period whose thought could not be confined by
these concepts. Some of these, including the later
Wittgenstein, emphasized considerably different and
broader approaches to the questions of truth and knowledge. Reference will be made later to some of these
broader perspectives. For the moment it is important
to continue to trace the influence of the positivists in
an effort to demonstrate its integral relationship to
some of the confusions in modern academic views of knowledge in social casework.

71

A. J. Ayer, the British empiricist, represented the view of logical positivism in his work which was studied extensively in this country. He clearly stated the positivist position that only statements of fact capable of verification by observation were to be considered meaningful. Everything else, with the exception of tautologies, was dismissed as nonsense.

> The criterion which we use to test the genuineness of apparent statements of fact is the criterion of verifiability. We say that a sentence is factually significant to any given person, if, and only if, he knows how to verify the proposition which it purports to express-- that is, if he knows what observations would lead him, under certain conditions, to accept the proposition as being true, or reject it as being false.
>
> . . .
>
> We enquire in every case what observations would lead us to answer the question, one way or the other; and, if none can be discovered, we must conclude that the sentence under consideration does not, as far as we are concerned, express a genuine question, however strongly its grammatical appearance may suggest that it does.[10]

Observation was the key to verifying a proposition. Difficulties, associated with decisions about what observations were to count as evidence so that a statement could be considered to be true if this evidence were found, were soon apparent. It was noted that in physics not everything can be directly observed and decisions were made about what would count as verification. For example, a vapor trail in a cloud chamber is accepted by physicists as evidence of the passage of electrons.

There were also problems with the inexactness characteristic of much language in common usage and an emphasis was placed upon the use of an empirical language. There have been some very complex efforts to analyze language which, as the foundation of all human intercourse, was inevitably involved in any effort to describe the kinds of evidence which would count to make a statement verifiable and hence meaningful.

Efforts to use the verifiability criterion produced a variety of situations which seemed to require further explication. In addition, if the verification criterion was in fact a universal requirement for the determination of meaningfulness, there was a need to ask what evidence would be considered acceptable to verify the verification criterion. A theory, however, cannot be used to verify itself. Eventually this need led to the statement that the verification criterion was really a proposal, in effect a recommendation.[11] The difficulties relating to verifying the theory itself were thus dissolved, rather than solved, since a recommendation does not need to be verified. However, a recommendation is just that. It can be studied in an effort to determine whether or not it is a good recommendation, a value judgment, but it no longer need be considered to be an authoritative statement that this represents the only way truths about the world can be known (in this case truths about meaningfulness).

Most efforts to make social work more scientific continue to emphasize verifiability in positivist terms. Much of the criticism of practice that it has not been proven to be effective is based upon positivist definitions of what would count to define and verify effectiveness.

The positivists assumed that science was able to establish what would count as verification for all statements which could be considered to be meaningful. This exaggerated view of the capabilities of science in effect elevates science to a position of omniscience and is basically the position of scientism which was discussed earlier. Science was thus to be the gate keeper regarding what matters were to be considered to have significance, what would count as verification, and what aspects of life would be acknowledged.

At least two additional problems were immediately evident. First, science itself is not omniscient and in fact is developing and changing.[12] From time to time the scientist's view of the world is revised to accord with new concepts. (It should also be noted that many theoretical advances in science come about as the result of intuitive and imaginative insights and it is often some time before methods of verification are found for these new scientific ideas.) Second, there are areas of human life not amenable to the use of scientific techniques, but meaningful nonetheless--areas which have traditionally been addressed in the humanities.

Many scientists, certainly most present day theoretical physicists, would not see this gate keeper role for everyone else as a valid extension of their role.

In modern society the specific area of a scientist's competence is apt to be quite circumscribed due to the complexity of the subjects studied and the resulting high degree of specialization which characterizes most scientific activity.

The verifiability requirement becomes even more problematical when it is extended into the area of knowledge about persons. There is doubt that science as presently constituted can assure reliability in knowing human beings. In psychology, for example, the behavioral theory, from which behavior modification techniques have developed, most nearly meets the positivist criterion of verifiability, but there are many aspects of human life not encompassed by this theory. Some of these aspects are discussed in subsequent chapters.

The primary point to be made here is that a reaction against both metaphysics and what was seen to be narrow religious dogma appears to have taken the form of what might be called a positivist dogma which is narrow and restrictive in a different way. This approach results in a tendency to see human beings as made up of mechanisms which a scientific technology will show how to manage so that they will function effectively. The question remains, however, of effectiveness to what purpose. What does it all mean anyway?

According to Smith:

Original positivism aimed, in the end, not at dealing constructively with the issues of religion and metaphysics but at eliminating them once and for all.[13]

It seems also to have eliminated any other kind of meaning in life which is not scientifically verifiable, thereby assigning most of the humanities--history, literature, art, as well as theology and most of philosophy--to the meaningless, or at least to the nonmeaningful.

Among the important aspects of human thought and life left out of this perspective of positivism was the presence of moral and ethical concerns which had historically belonged to philosophy. When required to address these issues:

The answer of positivism was a simple and straightforward subjectivism. All value

statements are emotive expressions: they do
not state something about an object but express how we feel about it. They are not
meaningless statements, but they are in no
sense cognitive.[14]

Difficulties quickly arose regarding this position
and it required reworking at various points. It is,
however, as mentioned earlier, preserved in attitudes
within social work whereby values and ethics are defined as preferences. For example, Levy says:

Values, to resort to a definition which is as
serviceable as any, are preferences with respect to which persons, groups, or societies
feel an 'affective regard.'

. . .

Ethics, although also a set of preferences
viewed with affective regard, connotes a
partiality toward particular forms, types
or manifestations of actions.[15]

Some discussions of values and ethics in the social
work literature are basically descriptive studies and
would not conflict with Ayer's statement that "ethics,
as a branch of knowledge, is nothing more than a department of psychology and sociology."[16] Most references in the social work literature, however, expect or
assume that social workers will subscribe to, i.e., prefer, certain specific values. The definition of values
as preferences, however, with the resultant tendency to
separate values from knowledge, which is seen to be
only that which is scientific, is basically a positivist
position.

It is remarkable that social work, involved as it
is with human lives as they are actually lived, could be
so influenced by a positivist view of the knowledge utilized in its practice. The separation of scientific,
objective facts (together with the thought which is
about them) and feeling (which is seen to be emotive,
noncognitive and subjective) is clearly a version of the
Cartesian dualism of the seventeenth century. In human
life thought and feeling are inextricably intertwined.
Even in science emotional connections provide the motive
power for much of the search for knowledge. Imaginative
ideas pursued with enthusiasm have lead to some of the
most creative contributions to science throughout the
centuries. It might also be noted that few philosophi-

cal arguments are carried on by positivists, or others, without the added impetus of an emotional commitment.

The scientists are rarely as dispassionate and objective as they appear to be to the positivists. Some complex techniques have been developed to correct for what is recognized as potential emotional bias on the part of researchers. It is not only in the sense of prejudice or bias, however, that emotions enter into scientific research. Intuition, imagination, and strong commitments are often, perhaps even usually, operative in the direcitons chosen to explore and the methods and approaches selected for these pursuits. The existence of these involvements is recognized by many of the most creative thinkers in the scientific field. For example, Holton says:

> Cases abound that give evidence of the role of 'scientific' preconceptions, passionate motivations, varieties of temperament, intuitive leaps, serendipity or sheer bad luck, not to speak of the incredible tenacity with which certain ideas have been held despite the fact that they conflicted with the plain experimental evidence, or the neglect of theories that would have quickly solved an experimental puzzle. None of these elements fit in with the conventional model of the scientist; they seem unlikely to yield to rational study; and yet they play a part in scientific work.[17]

The epistemology of physics, which is considered the paradigm for all knowledge by the positivists, has to a large extent moved beyond the positivist view of science. Einstein, whose discoveries began a major revolution in scientific thought, was at various points concerned with what could only be called metaphysical thinking. In a letter to Schlick in 1930 he said:

> In general, your presentation fails to correspond to my conceptual style insofar as I find your whole orientation so to speak too positivistic.
>
> . . .
>
> In short, I suffer under the (unsharp) separation of Reality of Experience and Reality of Being.[18]

Einstein's papers, as well as the recollections of those who worked with him, indicate that among the questions he was concerned with was, "What, precisely, is 'thinking'?"[19]

The thought of other physicists can also be used to illustrate the limits of positivism. Niels Bohr, whose work on the structure of the atom laid the groundwork for the quantum theory, is quoted as saying, "When it comes to atoms, language can be used only as in poetry. The poet, too, is not nearly so concerned with describing facts as with creating images."[20] Bronowski then says:

> When we step through the gateway of the atom, we are in a world which our senses cannot experience. There is a new architecture there, a way that things are put together which we cannot know: we only try to picture it by analogy, a new act of imagination. The architectural images come from the concrete world of our senses, because that is the only world that words describe. But all our ways of picturing the invisible are metaphors, likenesses that we snatch from the larger world of eye and ear and touch.[21]

The type of sense data on which the positivists depend has its roots in Descartes' strained efforts to separate the objective from the subjective in sense experience. Such a separation presents serious problems for the task of studying persons in social work, as indicated in subsequent chapters. Here the emphasis is upon its limitations for science itself. Heisenberg says:

> Natural science does not simply describe and explain nature; it is a part of the interplay between nature and ourselves; it describes nature as exposed to our method of questioning. This was a possibility of which Descartes could not have thought, but it makes the sharp separation between the world and the I impossible.[22] (Underlining added.)

Some of the ways the scientist is personally involved in his research are discussed in the next section in which Michael Polanyi's concept of personal knowledge is examined.

Footnotes

[1]Robert W. Roberts, Review of Effective Casework: An Eclectic Approach by Joel Fischer and The Task-Centered System by William J. Reid, in Social Casework 61 (May 1980):378.

[2]See, for example, Gordon, "Knowledge and Value: Their Distinction and Relationship in Clarifying Social Work Practice."

[3]Empiricism in philosophy is a broad term generally used to refer to the belief that experience is the foundation of all knowledge.

[4]William Barrett and Henry D. Aiken, eds., Philosophy in the Twentieth Century, 2 vols. (New York: Random House, 1962), 2:6.

[5]Book burning is fortunately in disrepute among modern intellectuals some of whom tend instead to use verbal techniques such as ridicule, derision and subtle innuendo directed against opposing views.

[6]Barrett and Aiken, 2:3.

[7]Ironically, in writing of the skepticism associated with Hume the physicist Werner Heisenberg says Hume "denied induction and causation and thereby arrived at a conclusion which if taken seriously would destroy the basis of all empirical science." See Physics and Philosophy (New York: Harper Torchbook, 1962), p. 84.

[8]Barrett, Illusion of Technique, p. 36.

[9]Ludwig Wittgenstein, quoted in Ibid., p. 33.

[10]A. J. Ayer, "The Elimination of Metaphysics," in Philosophy in the Twentieth Century, ed. Barrett and Aiken, 2:54.

[11]Carl Hemple, "Problems and Changes in the Empiricist Criterion of Meaning," in Philosophical Problems of Science and Technology, ed. Alex C. Michalos (Boston: Allyn & Bacon, 1974), pp. 314-315.

See, for example, Lewis Thomas, "On the Uncertainty of Science," _Harvard Magazine_ (September-October 1980):19-22.[12]

John E. Smith, _Themes in American Philosophy_ (New York: Harper Torchbooks, 1970), p. 188.[13]

Barrett and Aiken, _Philosophy in the Twentieth Century_, 2:9.[14]

Charles S. Levy, _Values and Ethics for Social Work Practice_ (Washington, D.C.: National Association of Social Workers, 1979), p. 1.[15]

A. J. Ayer, "Critique of Ethics and Theology," in Barrett and Aiken, _Philosophy in the Twentieth Century_, 2:95.[16]

Holton, _Thematic Origins of Scientific Thought_, p. 18.[17]

Albert Einstein, Letter to Moritz Schlick on 28 November 1930, quoted in Holton, p. 243.[18]

Ibid., p. 15.[19]

Bronowski, _The Ascent of Man_, p. 340.[20]

Ibid.[21]

Heisenberg, _Physics and Philosophy_, p. 81[22]

CHAPTER VII

PERSONAL KNOWLEDGE AND THE TACIT DIMENSION

The two interrelated concepts, personal knowledge and the tacit dimension, in Michael Polanyi's thought have particular relevance to the discussion here.[1] Polanyi (1891-1976) studied and taught in a variety of fields, including medicine, physical chemistry, the social sciences and philosophy, particularly the philosophy of science. His last book, written with the collaboration of Prosch, is Meaning and in many ways is the culmination of his thought as it applies to the situation in the modern western world.[2] A major thrust in his writing has been an effort to expand understanding of the nature of knowledge beyond the confines of positivism, which he saw as not only excessively limiting, but also as mistaken in its influence in both science and the humanities.

Personal knowledge refers to the idea that all knowledge involves the personal participation of the knower. The effort to objectify knowledge as though it were something out there and apart from the knower is seen as "a popular fallacy," destructive in its consequences. In Polanyi's thought when science is described in positivist terms it becomes a kind of mechanical reductionism which can be subverted in many ways, some of which endanger humanity. When human beings are reduced to automatons governed only by appetites and instincts, personal responsibility is not acknowledged and science can be used, often brutally, in the service of totalitarianism.[3]

It is important to emphasize that for Polanyi this perspective is based upon a mistaken idea of science,-- an idea which has left out a recognition of science as a human endeavor. Polanyi is particularly concerned with scientific research, with the areas in which the scientist seeks to extend the frontiers of knowledge, the truth seeking role of science. He believed that what is accepted as knowledge is in actuality personal knowledge, in which there is an integral and inevitable relationship between what is known and the knowing person. There is also for Polanyi an inescapable tacit dimension in all knowledge. He says, "All knowledge falls into one of these two classes: it is either tacit or rooted in tacit knowledge."[4]

The concept of tacit knowing is complicated and contains possibilities for enlightening the study of practice as well as the related activities of scientific research in social work.

The tacit dimension involves seeing knowledge as having three essential components. The knowing person focuses on something and integrates two kinds of aware- ness-focal and subsidiary. The subsidiary content, al- so described as "from-to," or "from-at," is a necessary part of all understanding. What is tacitly known in this subsidiary way can be at various levels of abstrac- tion. Focusing on the subsidiaries, however, can re- sult in a loss of the focal knowledge. One example used by Polanyi is that of a concert pianist. The pia- nist is usually only subsidiarily aware of what his fingers are doing. If he shifts his focus to the move- ments of his fingers, the ability to express the music is lost. It can be regained by shifting the focus back to the music, but the awareness of what the fingers are doing disappears into their subsidiary function. The important point is that, "The relation of a subsidiary to the focus is formed by the act of a person who inte- grates one to the other."[5]

These ideas make use of Gestalt psychology in empha- sizing how a focus on a whole configuration is different from an understanding of the parts viewed separately. One example is the picture seen through a stereo viewer which gives a quite different perspective from that seen when the two pictures are looked at separately. One sees the stereo picture but is also subsidiarily aware of the separate pictures which one is looking through to make the stereo picture.

In another example Polanyi refers to the way Gestalt psychology has described how it is possible to recognize the physiognomy of a person without being aware of the details which contribute to this recogni- tion. He says:

Gestalt psychology has assumed that perception of a physiognomy takes place through the spon- taneous equilibration of its particulars im- pressed on the retina of the eye or on the brain. However, I am looking at Gestalt, on the contrary, as the outcome of an active shaping of experience performed in the pursuit of knowledge. This shaping or integrating I hold to be the great and indispensable tacit power by which all knowledge is discovered and, once discovered, is held to be true.[6]

Another example frequently used by Polanyi is the way an object appears different when viewed at the end of a tube so that all peripheral clues are eliminated. A finger viewed in this fashion will appear to swell when moved closer, whereas without the tube the finger moved in the same way is perceived as retaining its shape and size. The reason for this is that the finger is seen in a context in which many clues point to its consistent reality. Clues of this kind are subsidiary and bear on the focus of the finger.

Subsidiary clues can be conscious, semiconscious, or unconscious. As previously indicated, some subsidiary clues can be identified and focused on--often with the loss of the focal meaning. Some subsidiary clues cannot be identified but contribute to a perception, or an intuition, so that a person "knows more than he can say," an important concept for Polanyi and one having relevance in social work practice. This kind of knowledge may provide guidance for the search for a hidden reality which is an important part of meaningful research.

Some things are known in a subsidiary way but cannot be described by the knower. One of the examples Polanyi has used to illustrate this aspect of tacit knowledge is a description of the experience of learning to ride a bicycle. One learns by the feel of it how to maintain one's balance, but this feel is part of a complex process.

The learner's imagination is fixed on the aim of keeping his balance, and this effort of the imagination implements its aim by subsidiarily evoking an observance of the rules that secure the cyclist's equilibrium: rules that would be useless to him if explicitly formulated.[7]

The cyclist is not aware of the complex processes which are integrated by the imagination. He uses his body in a subsidiary fashion, focusing on his goal of maintaining his balance. He is able to do this because he "dwells in" his body and in his developing knowledge of what it is necessary to do.

The concept of "dwelling in" is central in Polanyi's thought. It is by dwelling in various devices, including theories, that the mind extends itself into more complex ways of knowing and understanding. The mind uses parts of the body in this way and also uses tools and probes which are dwelt in as they become integrated

83

into the focal task of doing or learning something. Other knowledge can also be dwelt in as it is used to explore or understand. For example, Polanyi sees this kind of description as helpful in understanding how a theory is used to view what is being studied. In this case, a theory, through which one looks at aspects of the world in a search for meaning, he says, might be compared to eye glasses which help in the effort to see beyond themselves and can be used in this way only when they are not attended to as the focal point.

Polanyi's conception of how it is possible to know the mind of another is of particular interest to social work. He uses the example of a chess player seeking to understand the mind of a chess master.

> He does not <u>reduce</u> the master's mind to the moves the master makes. He dwells in these moves as subsidiary clues to the strategy in the master's mind which they enable him to see. The moves become meaningful at last only when they are seen to be integrated into a whole strategy. And a person's behavior, in general, becomes meaningful only when integrated into a whole mind.[8]

This way of "dwelling in" can be useful in understanding some of the process whereby a social worker comes to know the mind of another sufficiently to be able to help that person. It also suggests one of the limitations of a behavioristic approach, where behavior is viewed in a mechanical fashion and mechanistic devices are used in order to change it. <u>The behavior may in fact be changed, but in the light of Polanyi's concepts, if the person has been touched, it very likely will be because there was an unacknowledged tacit dimension in the helping process.</u> In fact, Polanyi says:

> Behaviorism tries to make psychology into an exact science. It professes to observe--i.e., <u>look at</u> pieces of mental behavior and to relate these pieces explicitly. But such pieces can be identified only within that tacit integration of behavior which behaviorists reject as unscientific. Thus the behaviorist analysis is intelligible only because it paraphrases, however crudely, the tacit integration which it pretends to replace.[9]

As the complexity of these ideas is developed, the way in which the person is involved in all knowledge becomes clearer. The search for knowledge is seen as a human effort to find coherence in the world. Intuition and imagination are found to utilize tacit knowledge, which cannot always be specified without destroying its way of bearing on that which is the center of attention or focus.

There is an essential indeterminancy about knowledge when understood in this way.

There is nothing in any concept that points objectively or automatically to any sort of reality. That a concept relates to a reality is established only by a tacit judgment grounded in personal commitments, and we are unable to specify all these personal commitments or to show how they bring a given concept to bear upon reality and thus enable us to trust it as knowledge. We are unable to do this because we are dwelling in these basic commitments and are unable to focus our attention upon them without destroying their subsidiary function.

.   .   .

Therefore, we cannot ultimately specify the grounds (either metaphysical or logical or empirical) upon which we hold that our knowledge is true. Being committed to such grounds, dwelling in them, we are projecting ourselves to what we believe to be true from or through these grounds. We cannot therefore see what they are. We cannot look at them since we are looking with them. They therefore must remain indeterminate.[10]

All knowledge, accepted and potential, is in these terms subject to error. The standards for judging error cannot be absolute. For Polanyi, in science it is primarily the community of scholars who must make judgments of what is a truthful, meaningful discovery. He also indicates that since it is not possible for each individual to have a grasp of all, or even most, areas of scientific knowledge, much that is commonly accepted is accepted on the basis of trust in the competence and integrity of the experts. And an expert opinion in science is in turn based upon a personal commitment, what Polanyi calls "a fiduciary act," on the part of the scientist.

This aspect of Polanyi's epistemology is useful for contemporary social work because it provides a deeper understanding of science and scientific discovery than that of positivism. Scientific research for Polanyi is seen as a quest for hidden meanings, an effort of discovery.

> It is personal, in the sense of involving the personality of him who holds it, and also in the sense of being, as a rule, solitary; but there is no trace in it of self-indulgence. The discoverer is filled with a compelling sense of responsibility for the pursuit of a hidden truth, which demands his services for revealing it. His act of knowing exercises a personal judgment in relating evidence to an external reality, an aspect of which he is seeking to apprehend.
>
> . . .
>
> To accept the pursuit of science as a reasonable and successful enterprise is to share the kind of commitments on which scientists enter by undertaking this enterprise. You cannot formalize the act of commitment, for you cannot express your commitment non-commitally.[11]

It is important also to note that scientific insights are subject to validation by others. The hidden meaning which is the object of the search is not a private knowledge, but one believed to have universal import and therefore subject to searching questioning and efforts at confirmation by others.

The relevance of tacit knowing to a liberal education has been addressed by Broudy. Most academic learning is evaluated by testing memory and the ability to repeat and apply in some detail the explicit content presented in course materials. While memory for detail recedes with the passage of time, it is Broudy's contention that what remains is tacit knowing--the ability to apply contexts and learned ways of approaching problems--what he calls the "associative and interpretive" uses of education. He says:

> There is reason to believe that persons who have studied certain disciplines the details of which they cannot recall nevertheless perform differently on reading and discussion tasks involving concepts from these disciplines than those who have not studied them.[12]

86

Broudy sees the importance of formal study of certain subjects as a means of providing subsidiary resources for the understanding of new focal material. He suggests that this concept be extended then to include a major goal of liberal education--that of developing in the mind of the knower "context-building resources."

Developing context-building resources can also be seen to be a part of the purpose of social work education in which students develop their ability to understand people who come from a wide variety of backgrounds and who often bring complex problems which have not been a part of the student's actual experience.

The concept of tacit knowing is also useful in understanding the function of intuition. While Polanyi's discussion refers primarily to intuition in scientific research, it has applicability to social work practice. The effort to understand another person which takes place in an interview utilizes tacit knowledge in several different ways. The social worker has a kind of fund of subsidiary information about how most people can be expected to respond in various situations, about what the external world, i.e., the environment, is probably like for this person, and tacit knowledge associated with the worker's own experiences as a human being. In addition, there is an active thrusting forward of the imagination, as Polanyi might say, on the worker's part in an effort to understand, and sometimes to mentally retrace, the experiences of the other person in terms of what it means to this particular human being. This involves an effort to know the mind of another person in the sense of understanding the meanings for that person of the experiences described, including the ways in which they are described.

The effort to understand is an effort to make sense out of the experiences described and is an active process in which intuition plays an important part. Intuition includes a subsidiary awareness of clues suggesting the direction for an inquiry (in science) and for the effort to understand in social work. The intuition grows out of subsidiary knowledge and, as in a scientific inquiry, efforts are made to follow leads so that what is experienced intuitively may be confirmed or discarded as the situation is further clarified. Intuition can thus be seen to play a vital, essential role in the effort to know another person.

Polanyi discusses language as "sense-giving" in that in communication words are selected because they have meanings which bear on what is being discussed. He notes that particular words lose their meaning when they are focused on directly and become only sounds or collections of letters. The meaning is restored when the focus returns to what the words are about. When experience is put into words this is "sense-giving." When the words are used to convey the experience to someone else it is called "sense-reading."[13] Sense-giving and sense-reading are essential to human discourse and come about because of sense-seeking, i.e., the search for coherence and meaning.

Polanyi pursues the study of language further, however, and explicates the way his theory of subsidiary and focal content, i.e., tacit knowing, can be applied to art. For example, regarding poetry he says,

> In other words, the rhythm, rhyme, sound, grammar, and all the other more subtle formal aspects of a poem, along with the several allusions of its parts, all jointly bear on the meaning of the poem. We are not therefore aware focally of what they add to that meaning and how they affect its quality.[14]

Polanyi's explication of the ways meanings are to be found in art suggests a dimension of social work which can best be understood as art and cannot be grasped by the use of the techniques of science. Efforts to confine descriptions of practice to variables which can be identified and isolated can destroy the process in which tacit knowledge is informing the focal effort to understand. The tacit dimension carried by the person of the social worker cannot be dissected out without losing the ability to enlighten the focal purpose of the interview. It is possible to study the tacit dimension in a focal way providing it is recognized and restored to its subsidiary role by a return to the original focus. Without this restoration the interview will have lost much of its purpose and will have become instead an exercise in manipulation. What is then being studied by means of isolated variables is something different from the complex effort of one human being to understand another--an effort enlightened by the tacit dimension and dependent upon human capacities to integrate different kinds of knowing.

While it is not necessary here to discuss extensively Polanyi's views with reference to the uses of metaphor and the functions of art, the following quotation with respect to drama may be helpful.

> Let us recall a similar paradox generated by a metaphor: the paradox that in a metaphor we say one thing and mean something else. We have a similar case in the theater. In witnessing a murder on the stage, we are aware of the setting and the antecedents of the stage murder, which are incompatible with the murder's being genuine; yet--just as in the case of the metaphor--we do not reject these contradictory affirmations, which would make the stage murder a nonsensical deception, but call upon our imaginative powers to integrate incompatible matters into a joint meaning. This joint meaning has, in a play, the peculiar quality of a dramatic event visible only to the imagination, just as the meaning of a metaphor, produced by the integration of its two incompatible constituents, is known to us only in our imagination.[15]

The function of the imagination in art as discussed above is relevant to these other ways of knowing which are necessary to the social work process. Without the use of imagination, the intuitive following of clues and the dwelling in language and another's experience, sense-giving and sense-reading, there would be no hope of understanding another mind or discovering what is needed by this particular human being. "And a person's behavior, in general, becomes meaningful only when integrated into a whole mind."

Footnotes

[1] See Michael Polanyi, <u>Personal Knowledge</u> (Chicago: University of Chicago Press, 1958, corrected edition 1962); and <u>The Tacit Dimension</u> (Garden City, New York: Doubleday 1966, Anchor Books 1967).

[2] Michael Polanyi and Harry Prosch, <u>Meaning</u> (Chicago: University of Chicago Press, 1975).
Excerpts from this book are reprinted by permission of the University of Chicago Press, Copyright 1975 by the University of Chicago.

[3]Ibid., p. 25.

[4]Michael Polanyi, Knowing and Being, edited by Marjorie Grune (Chicago: University of Chicago Press), p. 195.

[5]Polanyi and Prosch, Meaning, p. 38.

[6]Polanyi, The Tacit Dimension, p. 6.

[7]Polanyi, Knowing and Being, p. 200.

[8]Polanyi and Prosch, Meaning, p. 48.

[9]Polanyi, Knowing and Being, p. 152.

[10]Polanyi and Prosch, Meaning, p. 61.

[11]Polanyi, The Tacit Dimension, p. 25.

[12]Broudy, "Tacit Knowing as a Rationale for Liberal Education," p. 52.

[13]Polanyi, Knowing and Being, pp. 181-207.

[14]Polanyi and Prosch, Meaning, p. 80.

[15]Ibid., p. 83.

CHAPTER VIII

KNOWLEDGE OF THE PERSON--THE SELF AND OTHERS

The Nature of Being a Person

Human beings are characterized by the ability to reason and to develop and use, for thinking and communication, a variety of languages--verbal, mathematical, and artistic. These languages are the means of expression of all that is essentially human. They are used by persons for both cognitive and expressive purposes, and in efforts to understand the mixture of thought and feeling which makes up most of human experience. Attempts at precision in language are necessary, in fact vital to the consensually validated meanings required for communication. However, these efforts at precision, when used to describe human beings, as the previous discussion indicates, carry the possibility of destroying meaning by oversimplification--a risk which positivism demonstrates and which has particular significance for social casework, which is concerned with human beings in all their complexity.

Humans are self conscious beings, cognizant both of being and limitation. Human beings know that they die. For the individual, existence as known has a beginning and an end and the interim period is time limited. Even the concept of time is uniquely human. Limitation and the accompanying uncertainties are not always gracefully accepted, with the resultant hubris evident in assertions of personal infallibility or in various kinds of dogma in the guise of religion or science or sometimes a combination of the two. The awareness of limitation can also have an opposite effect--and lead to a despair of meaning.

Human beings question and seek meaning for their lives. Sometimes it is the confrontation with death or loss in some other form which stimulates the search. When life is basically comfortable, and prospects for the future hopeful and seemingly unlimited, mundane aspects of life often predominate and these human questions may lie dormant. Sooner or later, however, experiences of pain and suffering, loss and sorrow, are likely to bring questions about the meaning of life to the fore. For some fortunate few, perhaps securely lodged in a religious tradition, the experience is not so harrowing. Others, however, feel cut loose and lost and may seek or be brought for help. In these situations the search for meaning may be clearly evident or disguised, but the appeal comes in a person to person context. To the positivist scientist the question may well be meaningless, and hence not recognizable. To the questioner, however, it can be crucial.

Social work has long had a tradition which emphasizes starting where the client is. A too narrow philosophical framework, however, may place blinders on the worker, who is not then able to perceive the dimensions of a problem beyond its most literal expression.

Because humans are essentially social beings, lives and meanings are intertwined. No person can know who he is without reference to others. In addition, no person is truly confirmed except through his encounters with others. For most people purposefulness and usefulness are vital parts of the meaning of their lives and these are found in the community of other persons. Modern social work in accord with the cultural times may choose to use the term eco-systems to refer to both the physical and social environment. The risk, however, is that the choice of language may obscure the human.

Language is basically social. It is learned through experience, in the context of human relationships. The language of mathematics lends itself to the most precision, which can be seen to account for the way it is highly valued by the positivists. Mathematics can be said to be the language of logic. Verbal language as used in human discourse can also be logical, but as a rule is much less precise, but is also richer in its ability to express the wide range of human experience. Artistic languages are the least precise, but often communicate at levels for which no other language is adequate or often even available. Throughout life the self becomes known, insofar as it is known, primarily through verbal and artistic language and imagery. An awareness of the relevance of these dimensions of human life is therefore a necessary part of the person to person activity which makes up most of social work.

The Objective - Subjective Problem

As indicated earlier, the emphasis in much of science upon objective observations has led to a value judgment in social work that objective knowledge is superior to that which is subjective. Polanyi's idea of personal knowledge has been discussed in the previous chapter as a way of bridging this artificially created gap. The emphasis in Polanyi's thought is upon personal participation in a discovery which also becomes meaningful for others because it is seen as reflecting a hidden reality and is subject to examination by others. Holton makes a similar point when he distinguishes between what he sees as two aspects of science.

> One is the private aspect, science-in-the making, the speculative, perhaps largely nonverbal activity, carried on without self-consciously examined methods, with its own motivations, its own vocabulary, and its own modes of progress. The other is the public aspect, science-as-an-institution, the inherited world of clarified, codified, refined concepts that have passed through a process of scrutiny and have become part of a discipline that can be taught, no longer showing more than some traces of the individual struggle by which it had been originally achieved. This, roughly can be characterized as the difference between the 'subjective' and the 'objective' aspects of truth-seeking.[1]

For social work, however, there is an additional dimension to this problem. The social worker's self is very much involved in the process of helping others. One of the commonly accepted goals in learning social work is the "conscious use of self," which requires self discipline. Self discipline necessitates knowledge of the self. There can be no escaping this aspect of the involvement of the self in the social work process, particularly in direct practice. To deny it is simply not to recognize its presence. Social workers are often aware of what is called personal style in their work. The expression personal style really says, in effect, that this is how I can best use who I am in the social work relationship with this other person.

Knowledge of the self is closely related to the concept of personal identity, which often does receive attention in social work, for example, through study of Erikson. The study of the self is also a part of ego psychology which is based upon Freud's work but includes different emphases.[2] In much of the literature of ego psychology, however, the term "object" continues to be used to refer to a person, as in the "love object" in Freudian theory, sometimes making it difficult to recognize that it is persons who are being talked about. As suggested earlier, Freud felt it was important to be scientific and similar concerns continue into the present. Some of the later theorists, such as Erikson,

have sought to correct the problem by the use of terminology more in accord with the reciprocity of human relationships, which is now recognized as beginning as
early as infancy.

The study of the self, however, in social work is
often still entangled in the subjective-objective emphasis of Cartesian dualism associated with a positivist
philosophy. In its research activities social work requires an expanded view of the philosophy of science
such as has been suggested in the earlier discussion,
but more than this is necessary. Social work in practice
needs a philosophical framework broad enough to encompass all that is human.

It is important to emphasize the damaging effects
within the field of social work of this subjective-
objective dichotomy originating with Descartes, particularly with reference to sense data. As indicated in
the earlier discussion of positivism, the effort to
assign sense data to the objective world confronts the
fact that what is known from human sense experience is
known internally. If the world is divided into what is
objective, i.e., outside the person, and what is subjective or internal, sense experience then belongs to
the subjective world. Descartes resolved this dilemma
by assigning that part of sense experience which can
be dealt with in a mathematical way to the external
world--that is, those observations which can be measured
by instruments which are available to any interested observer.

Modern positivist scientists continue to speak of
sense data as if it had this kind of objective, out
there, quality. For example, a dictionary of sociology
includes in its definition of scientific method:

> The scientific method is based on the assump-
> tion that knowledge is based on what is ex-
> perienced through the senses, and that if a
> statement concerning natural phenomenon is to
> be accepted as meaningful or true it must be
> empirically verifiable.[3]

Under empiricism in the same dictionary the first definition given is that of philosophy that all knowledge
is based on experience. The second definition is given
as follows:

> In science, the view that generalizations can
> be held to be valid only when tested by ob-

jective techniques and verified by sense experience. Empiricism is based on the belief that only that which can be experienced by the senses is real and that the final test of scientific truth is the experience of the senses....Such observations, however, must be shared by qualified persons in the discipline, and not be idiosyncratic.[4]

Careful examination of these definitions discloses the dilemmas of the Cartesian dualism. If the world is material, mass, res extensa, then these definitions seem to have coherence. However, the concern with avoiding the idiosyncratic is an implicit recognition of the subjectivism of sense experience, that it actually belongs to the world of mind, res cogitans. Science has sought to avoid this problem through emphasis upon intersubjective agreement on the part of the observers. It is notable that the word is intersubjective. It is, however, considered to be most accurate when the agreement refers to instrument readings and measurements.

In many aspects of the material world, particularly with reference to technological matters, these methods are useful and appropriate. There are, however, other areas in which they can be seen to be inadequate. Modern physics has come to view the world differently, as indicated in the earlier discussion. Other physicists in addition to Heisenberg might be mentioned here. Born, for example, commented that physics had become philosophy.

Bronowski says:

Max Born meant that the new ideas in physics amount to a different view of reality. The world is not a fixed, solid array of objects, out there, for it cannot be fully separated from our perception of it. It shifts under our gaze, it interacts with us, and the knowledge it yields has to be interpreted by us. There is no way of exchanging information that does not demand an act of judgment.

. . .

...whatever fundamental units the world is put together from, they are more delicate, more fugitive, more startling than we can catch in the butterfly net of our senses.[5]

The complexity of the way human sense experience leads to knowledge becomes apparent through the work of the modern physicists. It should not, however, require physics to tell social work that knowledge and understanding of human beings is intricate and much influenced by the way sense experience is mediated and interpreted in the human mind. Positivistic science is involved in various peregrinations in an effort to guarantee objectivity from subjectively experienced data. Again it should be emphasized that the resulting techniques serve appropriate technological purposes in the world. A profession whose business is understanding human beings, however, needs a philosophy broad enough to encompass all that is truly human and which does not require an effort to separate sense experience from the experiencing person.

Efforts to deal with this matter in the literature of social work sometimes appear to be a problem of vocabulary, i.e., using the same word but with a somewhat different meaning. For example, Perlman seems to be making an effort to retain the word objectivity for social work, but to shift its usage away from positivistic definitions. She says:

Objectivity is an act of conscious discipline and self-management.[6]

Objectivity is attained and maintained not by a detachment from the material with which one works--whether it is people or particles--but by awareness and discipline of self in the interests of the quest.[7]

'Objectivity' is the recognition and then the management or control of one's subjectivity.[8]

These efforts to define objectivity can be seen to be efforts to struggle with duality in human life, but a duality defined differently from that of Descartes and his successors in positivism. If pushed to the extreme the original problem is the same--i.e., the question of the existence of a world apart from the observing person. The problem is, however, that there is no knowledge of such an existent world apart from knowing persons.

Perlman's definitions seem to reflect an acceptance of a concept of existence found in those modern philosophers concerned with the integral relationship between being and knowing. (A philosophical perspective also

evident in the thought of some modern physicists as indicated in the earlier discussion.) Philosophies which
grapple with this relationship assume the possibility
of common knowledge, i.e., knowledge which can be understood and often confirmed by others as well as the self.
The separation from the positivists comes as a result of
the recognition that what is known is known ultimately
only through the mediation of the person, who integrates
sense impressions, perceptions and ascribed meanings.
All this takes place in a social context in which consensually validated meanings are then accepted as reality. But what is thus known is not knowledge of an
outside world whose reality is uncontaminated by the
human mind as the positivists seem to seek. It is
rather knowledge of the world as mediated by mind. One
can assume the existence of an objective, out there
world, perhaps, but one cannot know it directly. As
Polanyi says:

> We are told that the consciousness of another
> person is not directly observed but merely in-
> ferred from external facts, and that a strict
> empiricism prefers to acknowledge only facts
> that are directly observed. But nothing is
> ever observed except by the aid of intelligent
> transactions which integrate a great number of
> impacts made on our several senses along with
> the internal responses evoked by these impacts
> within our own body. What we see and hear de-
> pends in a thousand ways on the preparedness of
> our own mind and on our intelligent participa-
> tion in making out what it is that we see and
> hear.[9]

All of this becomes more complicated but also more
significant for social work when the discussion centers
on the question of the relationship between persons
which concerns Perlman and which for many, perhaps most,
social workers is an integral part of their activities.

On Relationship

The importance of the relationship between social
worker and the person served has long been recognized.
In the history of social work it has been frequently
mentioned and often discussed. Perlman notes, however,
an apparent lessening of interest in this subject in the
recent literature.[10] For example, in Abstracts for
Social Workers between 1968 and 1978 she found no listing for the topic of relationship, although there are
references, primarily in publications in psychology, to

97

related terms such as empathy. Also she comments on the cursory treatment in some of the commonly used text-books.[11]

Perlman attributes this apparent diminution of interest to the possibility that current authors feel the subject has been adequately covered, or exhausted, by the earlier emphasis in the field. The concerns expressed here suggest another possible interpretation for this curtailed treatment of a traditionally recognized aspect of social work. This shift in interest away from concepts of relationship might be ascribed to the emphasis upon positivistic science in academic social work during this period. Such an interpretation certainly could be given to the definition quoted by Perlman from the Pincus and Minahan book whereby relationship is seen as "an affective bond between the worker and other systems."[12]

Evident in these references to the literature is the continuing debate within social work which is most evident in the academic and practice areas with reference to objective data and practice wisdom. Questions about the nature of data described as objective have already been discussed and continue to be a theme throughout the rest of this discussion.

Practice wisdom is an ambiguous term, sometimes used pejoratively for aspects of social work activity not readily translatable into positivist terms. In this sense the term is used to apply to what is seen as subjective, intuitive interpretations of the social worker with the implicit assumption that these interpretations are suspect because they cannot be objectively analyzed. It is proposed here that aspects of what has been called practice wisdom should be studied and submitted to disciplined efforts to understand what is involved in it. It is suggested that this is one important area where efforts to reduce the discussion to positivistic terms have the effect of either destroying much that is integral to the practice of social work[13] or leaving these aspects to operate sub rosa rather than in an appropriately disciplined way. The objective-subjective dichotomy can be seen to be particularly dysfunctional with reference to this aspect of social work.

There have been efforts to study the concept of relationship by scientific methods. Such studies have usually been under the aegis of clinical psychology and in the context of psychotherapy. The most notable projects in this area have been those having their origins in Rogers' work, which has been developed and explicated by Truax and Carkhuff[14] and Barrett-Lennard.[15] The terms used by Rogers in his studies were "genuineness or congruence-realness, caring or unconditional positive regard, and accurate empathic understanding,"[16] and the Truax and Carkhuff variations were "accurate empathy, nonpossessive warmth, and genuineness."[17] Many of these studies have demonstrated a correlation between these conditions and reported positive outcomes in psycho-therapy.[18] These studies are useful in identifying some aspects of relationship as it is usually used with reference to social work. There is some disagreement about the meanings in practice of such terms as unconditional positive regard, but this does not diminish the importance of the effort to understand something of the human qualities which are helpful in a therapeutic relationship.

In 1955 Rogers wrote of his personal struggle to integrate his beliefs in the importance of the most subjective aspects of the therapeutic relationship with his convictions about the value and usefulness of science. He called attention to the subjective aspects of science and the role of scientific techniques in efforts to avoid self deception. He said:

> Thus scientific methodology is seen for what it truly is--a way of preventing me from deceiving myself in regard to my creatively formed subjective hunches which have developed out of the relationship between me and my material.
>
>   .   .   .
>
> The splendid structure of science rests basically upon its subjective use by persons. It is the best instrument we have yet been able to devise to check upon our organismic sensing of the universe.[19]

The efforts to study those aspects of relationship which contribute to effective psychotherapy usually depend upon the previously mentioned concepts of inter-subjective validation. It seems important to note again these subjective aspects of science and to emphasize that the Cartesian dichotomy accepted by positivism results in an unduly limited view of what constitutes science. This underlying problem can be seen in efforts to study objectively, and to measure, the qualities which are involved in a helping relationship.

In order to deepen an understanding of relationship

with reference to social work, it is necessary to return to the earlier discussion of what it means to be
a person. Relationship is a vital part of social work
because it is a vital part of human life. Human life
is lived in a social context, which determines to a
large extent the ways persons think, how they view themselves and others, and what they consider to be essential to existence.

The importance of relationships from earliest infancy, beginning with the first nurturing person, is becoming increasingly evident in recent studies such as
those reported by Fraiberg.[20] Much earlier studies by
John Bowlby have shown that infants either do not sur-
vive at all or are seriously damaged in their development where this early nurturing relationship is missing.[21] Recent studies by Brazelton have indicated that
infants recognize and respond to these nurturing persons much earlier than had previously been realized.[22]

It has of course long been known that learning
takes place in a social context. The significance of
the way this permeates all of human life has not always
been acknowledged, however. For example, Polanyi says:

> We acquire our naturalistic system of explana-
> tions as we first acquire speech, uncritically
> absorbing the idiom of our elders.
>
> .   .   .
>
> We are born into a language, and we are also
> born into a set of beliefs about the nature
> of things. And, once brought up in our be-
> liefs, we embrace them with sufficient con-
> viction to participate in imposing them on
> the next generation. We wager our lives on
> these beliefs, and we share in building on
> these beliefs the life of the whole commu-
> nity which holds them.[23]

Out of this social matrix into which one is born,
and within which one develops, grows a personal sense of
self and of what is necessary and acceptable in a society of other selves. Throughout life other selves continue to be of vital importance to the individual no
matter how isolated he may appear to be.

In a discussion of the meaning of being a responsible self, H. Richard Niebuhr speaks of "man's long
quest after knowledge of himself as agent--that is, as

a being in charge of his conduct,"24 and he emphasizes the social nature of this being.

> Without obscuring the fact that the self exists as a rational being in the presence of ideas, or exists as moral being in the presence of mores and laws, this view holds in the center of attention the fundamentally social charac-ter of selfhood. To be a self in the presence of other selves is not a derivative experience but primordial.

. . .

> ...the exploration of this dimension of self existence has taken place in many areas of modern man's thinking; many lines of inquiry have converged on the recognition that the self is fundamentally social, in this sense that it is a being which not only knows it-self in relation to other selves but exists as self only in that relation.25

The primordial nature of relationship26 is expli-cated in the work of Martin Buber whose terms I-Thou and I-It have been widely accepted, although not always in ways which do justice to the depth of his thought. In his book, I and Thou,27 published in 1923 and avail-able in English since 1937, Buber writes of the intrin-sic nature of I-Thou and I-It relationships in human life. The I-It refers to the relationship of the self to objects which may be either material objects, in-tellectual concepts, or other people who, by being treated as objects, lose their personal character. The I-Thou relationship refers to the living mutual re-lationship that comes about between persons. The em-phasis is upon the meeting of persons as very different from using and manipulating which belong to the world of I-It.

For Buber the I-Thou relationship is rooted in man's relationship to the eternal Thou. This theologi-cal dimension is essential to an understanding of Buber's thought and further reference is made to this in the later discussion. For the present, however, the focus here is upon how the self exists in relationship to the world of other selves. For Buber the monad is expressed by the hyphenated word I-Thou, which is mistakenly in-terpreted as a dyad. This view represents a basic quali-tative difference between the view of the psychologists in the research mentioned earlier that relationship can best be understood by separating out various identifiable elements located in one participant. The integrity of the I-Thou relationship may be destroyed by this effort and the relationship become that of I-It. Buber says:

> In the beginning is relation--as category of being readiness, grasping form, mould for the soul; it is the a priori of relation, the inborn Thou.[28]

In the meeting between I and Thou there is movement and change and spontaneity--but no interference or exertion of control of one self over another. A true I-Thou relationship cannot be sustained indefinitely and human beings are drawn back into the world of I-It, the world of material objects, where people are also often treated as objects. Buber calls this the two-fold nature of man, referring to the way in which this back and forth movement between I-Thou and I-It takes place.[29]

This back and forth movement can be seen to be an essential part of the social work process. Many concepts used in social work belong to the world of I-It, for example, such psychoanalytic concepts as transference and countertransference. Often it is necessary to understand the ways persons continue to respond to people in the present on the basis of previous experiences with others who were important to them earlier in life. Skillful use of such understanding can open the way to the development of an I-Thou relationship. If these possible influences from the past are not recognized by the social worker, however, the old circular, often destructive, patterns may well continue uninterrupted, perhaps even reinforced by the worker's unknowing participation.

In social work practice the purpose of the relationship is to further the well being of the other and Buber's thought is helpful in understanding how this is possible. He says:

> For the inmost growth of the self is not accomplished, as people like to suppose today, in man's relation to himself, but in the relation between the one and the other, between men, that is, pre-eminently in the mutuality of the making present--in the making present of another self and in the knowledge that one is made present in his own self by the other-- together with the mutuality of acceptance, of affirmation and confirmation.[30]

102

As a result of interest shown in his writings Buber also dealt with how a therapeutic relationship, and sometimes an educational one, can be possible in the sense of I-Thou, despite certain restraints upon the therapist or teacher. Such a relationship cannot be full in its mutuality in that the interest of both participants necessarily center on the needs of only one.[31]

In writing about relationship in social work, for those just starting as well as those with experience, Perlman says:

> How can you 'relate'--which is to say, so act in the helping interchange--that the person you assist may experience some sense of being cared about by another human being and of being allied with him? He will not be asking you for a relationship. He is likely to be asking for some plain, ordinary, necessary life-sustaining thing like money, like medicine, like advice, like action in his behalf. But what he gets from you, whether in material or psychological form, will be 'twice blessed' when it is conveyed in such a way as to affirm his personal worth and his social linkage.[32]

The above quotation from the social work literature suggests the way in which relationship in social work has its roots in caring which, in its motivation and the ways it is expressed, is essentially a moral principle. In fact, caring can be seen to be a basic moral principle for social work, i.e., a basic good which social work practice is designed to implement.

Relationship and caring are integrally related and yet receive little attention in much of the current social work literature. The omissions regarding these concepts may reflect an ambivalence in the profession toward issues which cannot be readily encompassed by a positivist philosophy. As suggested earlier, two possible attitudes might be found to explain the apparent lack of interest. One is that given by Perlman that somehow the concepts are deemed to have been dealt with and are now taken for granted. The second possibility is that they are not considered really important since they are difficult if not impossible to study by present empirical methods.[33] At times both attitudes appear to exist side by side and there is often a kind of embarrassment associated with the use of words such as caring and goodness.

Footnotes

[1]Holton, _Thematic Origins of Scientific Thought_,
p. 15.

[2]See, for example, the concept of ego strength in
Howard J. Parad and Roger R. Miller, eds., _Ego-Oriented
Casework_ (New York: Family Service Association of
America, 1963), and Howard J. Parad, ed., _Ego Psycho-
logy and Dynamic Casework_ (New York: Family Service
Association, 1958).

[3]George A. Theodorson and Achilles G. Theodorson,
Modern Dictionary of Sociology (New York: Thomas Y.
Crowell, 1969), p. 370.

[4]_Ibid._, p. 131.

[5]Bronowski, _The Ascent of Man_, p. 364.

[6]Perlman, _Relationship_, p. 58.

[7]_Ibid._, footnote, p. 58.

[8]_Ibid._, p. 59.

[9]Michael Polanyi, "Scientific Thought and Social
Reality: Essays by Michael Polanyi," ed. by Fred
Schwartz, _Psychological Issues_ VIII, Monograph 32 (New
York: International Universities Press, 1974):140-41.

[10]Perlman, _Relationship_, Notes, pp. 219-220.

[11]She mentions specifically, Allen Pincus and Anne
Minahan, _Social Work Practice: Model and Method_ (Otasca,
Ill.: F.E. Peacock, 1973); Carol Meyer, _Social Work
Practice_ (New York: Free Press, 1976); and Briar and
Miller, _Problems and Issues in Social Casework_.

[12]Perlman, _Relationship_, p. 220.

[13]See, for example, the earlier discussion of the
tacit dimension in Chapter VIII.

[14]Truax and Carkhuff, _Toward Effective Counseling and Psychotherapy: Training and Practice_.

[15]G. T. Barrett-Lennard, "Dimensions of Therapists Response as Causal Factors in Therapeutic Change," _Psychological Monographs_ 76 (1962):1-33.

[16]Rogers and John K. Wood, "Client Centered Theory: Carl R. Rogers, in _Operational Theories of Personality_, ed. Arthur Burton, pp. 211-258.

[17]Truax and Carkhuff, _Toward Effective Counseling and Psychotherapy: Training and Practice_.

[18]Alan S. Gurman, "The Patient's Perception of the Therapeutic Relationship," in _Effective Psychotherapy, a Handbook of Research_, eds. Alan S. Gurman and Andrew M. Razin (London: Pergamon Press, 1977), pp. 503-543.

[19]Carl R. Rogers, "Persons or Science? A Philosophical Question," _The American Psychologist_ 10 (1955): 275.

[20]Selma Fraiberg, ed., _Clinical Studies in Infant Mental Health, The First Year of Life_ (New York: Basic Books, 1980).

[21]John Bowlby, _Maternal Care and Mental Health_ (Geneva: World Health Organization, 1951).

[22]See, for example, T. Berry Brazelton, _On Becoming a Family_ (New York: Delacorte Press, 1981).

[23]Polanyi, "Scientific Thought and Social Reality," p. 75.

[24]H. Richard Niebuhr, _The Responsible Self_, with an Introduction by James F. Gustafson (New York: Harper & Row, 1963), p. 48.

[25]_Ibid._, p. 71.

[26]_Ibid._, p. 72.

[27]Martin Buber, I and Thou, 2nd ed., trans. Ronald Gregor Smith (New York: Charles Scribners Sons, 1958).

[28]Ibid., p. 27.

[29]Ibid., p. 3.

[30]Martin Buber, The Knowledge of Man, trans. with an introduction by Maurice Friedman (New York: Harper & Row, 1965), p. 71.

[31]For a discussion of this point see "Dialogue between Martin Buber and Carl R. Rogers," in The Knowledge of Man, pp. 169-172.

[32]Perlman, Relationship, p. 19.

[33]With reference to some of the difficulties associated with efforts to study therapeutic relationships, see Kevin M. Mitchell, Jerold D. Bozarth, and Conrad C. Kraupt, "A Reappraisal of the Therapeutic Effectiveness of Accurate Empathy, Nonpossessive Warmth, and Genuineness," in Effective Psychotherapy, A Handbook of Research, eds. Gurman and Razin, pp. 482-502.

CHAPTER IX

MORAL PHILOSOPHY

The word moral is especially troublesome for modern
social workers. The major difficulty is probably related to the historical origins of social work in the
charity organization societies which were often concerned with making judgments about the worthiness of
those in need. There are also difficulties when the
word is used to express ideological preferences such as
the contemporary "moral majority" movement.

Despite these culturally based abuses and the re-
servations they engender, it is suggested here that
social work is intrinsically involved with moral issues
and that the word moral should be reclaimed by the profession in the basic meanings it has in philosophy.
Moral philosophy is concerned with what is good, or
evil, or somewhere in between--with what is valued--
and what people ought to do--with what is ethical.

At various points throughout the discussion here
two themes in modern social work have been noted--i.e.,
the search for relevant knowledge and the values and
moral commitments of the profession. These two themes
appear to be poorly integrated in the profession and
reasons for this lack of integration may be found in
the effort to limit the definition of knowledge to that
which is scientific, and to consign values and moral
commitments to the realm of preferences, with the implication that this is essentially a personal matter
without any particular justification. It has been suggested that these definitions reflect the influence of
positivist thinking which has been found to be inadequate for the physical sciences and is even more un-
satisfactory for understanding the human problems with
which social work is concerned.

In addition to the kinds of knowledge which have
already been discussed, it is now argued that it is possible to know, not just to prefer, what is good and
valuable and also to seek knowledge about what this
means in practice for those who would do social work.

This issue has recently been addressed by Reamer.
He calls attention to the way in which social work has
traditionally stated its values, but for the most part
has not dealt with how these values are justified or
how generally accepted ethical principles are to be
applied.[1] In his discussion Reamer defines some of the

terms and outlines the various positions which are to be found in some philosophical theories which provide the foundation for deciding ethical issues. He argues for the particular theory of Alan Gewirth called "the principle of generic consistency," as a supreme moral principle. This principle, similar in some respects to the Golden Rule, considers all human beings to have fundamental rights to "freedom and well being."[2] Reamer's work is an important contribution, not necessarily because of the details of the specific position he advocates, but because it is the first systematic effort to apply the principles of ethical reasoning to values and ethics in social work.

There is a problem, however, in regard to Reamer's use of the term intuition with reference both to ethical theory and to practice wisdom in social work. Basically it is a question of semantics and illustrates some of the pitfalls associated with interdisciplinary work in which in different disciplines the same words may have somewhat different connotations.[3]

In his conclusions Reamer comments on the complexity of the issues in practice.

> Practitioners' intuition, or practice wisdom, and the results of empirical research should continue to serve as important sources of information for making ethical decisions. It should be recognized, however, that practitioners will disagree about what both practice wisdom and empirical data suggest ought to be done in particular cases, and thus they cannot be relied on for clear ethical standards.[4]

The basic questions he says are judgments about how "the freedom and well being of clients will best be safeguarded and promoted."[5]

Underlying principles in social work on which most practitioners and researchers can agree would appear to be freedom and the well being of clients, by whatever line of reasoning these are justified--and there are a variety of possibilities utilizing the thought of many of the major western philosophers. It is suggested here that caring is a fundamental moral principle which in effect motivates social workers to be concerned about the freedom and well being of others.

Most discussions of social work in which the thinking of philosophers has played an integral part have emanated from Great Britain. For example, the International Library of Welfare and Philosophy series includes papers by social workers and philosophers on self-determination.[6] An earlier work also published in England by Raymond Plant discusses the philosophical meaning of the dual concern of social casework with individuals and their social roles. He calls attention to the way concern with individuals and their social relationships has political ramifications. He seems to arrive at a position which has engaged social work from its earliest days, that is, the idea that primary effort should be devoted to changing society to make it more compatible with individual needs. Plant's discussion is important in the way in which philosophical thought is brought to bear on the problem, but in his particular line of reasoning the focus is shifted from the individual to society. He says in conclusion:

> These are models and possibilities; it is not for the philosopher qua philosopher to recommend one or the other, rather to try to understand the presuppositions and implications of theories, in this case with reference to casework. What is clear, however, is that implicitly at least the theory and practice of social casework raise in an immediate and important manner some of the most difficult problems of social and political theory.[7]

The point to be made here is that the nature of society is an important focus for all social workers. However, the need to understand moral involvements and commitments and how these are implemented in practice cannot be dissolved in the broader social issues which remain of concern, but are not the primary focus of direct practice with persons in need.

Another author, a casework practitioner, himself, has focused on the social worker in public agencies in England. Jordan discusses some of the dilemmas which confront the worker in these settings.

> The point about the services I am concerned with is that they can only be good services if they are given in a certain way--sensitively, and with a generous offer of individual attention. They are no less part of the Welfare State for this, and they should be available to all who need them. Yet the detailed means by which they are given are as important as their organization and planning, and these

two aspects of their provision are often
closely linked in problematic ways.

What I am suggesting is that social work help
is not so much a service in itself as a way
of giving certain services. Without this in-
gredient, these services will not be of good
quality, no matter how well they are organized.[8]

Philosophical discussions between practitioners,
such as Jordan, and philosophers, such as Plant and
others, are needed in order to identify and explore the
interweaving of philosophical issues in social work
practice. This is essentially an interdisciplinary project and requires that persons in the different disciplines of philosophy and social work seek to understand
the frames of reference, and vocabulary, of each other.

The interdisciplinary work which has been done in
ethics and medicine in recent years has relevance here
and some of the principles found to be useful there are
also relevant to philosophy and social work. There
are certain problems concerning the use of langugae.
There is a need to consciously avoid jargon which tends
to be more habitual than realized when communication
takes place within a profesison.

Jargon is not the main problem, however. Cassell
comments that people can ask about words they do not
understand, but that greater difficulties arise when
people do not realize that the same words may have different meanings in different professions.[9] This problem can complicate efforts to deal with philosophical
issues in social work. There are many words used by
various philosophers with meanings widely divergent from
those conventionally accepted within social work--words
like reality and existence, for example.

Some of the problems with language occur because of
the differing frames of reference of various disciplines,
and for Cassell the shift, often difficult and painful,
to a broader frame of reference is the mark of success-
ful interdisciplinary work.

Slowly dawning but then suddenly clear, the
frame of reference enlarges. For me, it was
coming to see medicine as existing within the
much larger system of the moral life of mankind. I do not mean merely the realization
that there is a world outside of medicine

(although that, too, could be a first and
vital change in a frame of reference). Rather,
I realized that understanding in moral philosophy is fundamental to understanding medicine.
With that change, what other participants had
to say became not merely something I would have
liked to understand in order to broaden my
knowledge of the world, but rather something I
realize that I <u>must</u> understand so that I can
bring order back into my comprehension of medicine. The point is, of course, that with the
enlargement of the frame of reference, the previous structure of my comprehension of medicine
has become uncertain and the new knowledge from
other disciplines is not merely useful but
necessary to restore stability to the conceptual
structure.[10]

Something akin to Cassell's experience may be necessary for social workers in order to address moral issues
which underlie practice. Philosophical language and the
complexities of the thought of the various philosophers
are difficult for social workers. Some of the reasons
for this, in addition to those discussed here, have
been mentioned in previous chapters. If philosophical
problems in social work are to be analyzed, however,
some practitioners must be involved in the process. If
they are not, any results of such analyses will have
limited relevance for actual practice.

While all social workers cannot be, nor do they
wish to be, involved, those who participate in interdisciplinary efforts can serve as translators for
others--much as Reamer is doing in his recent contributions to the social work literature. Such interdisciplinary efforts militate against the oversimplifica-
tions which result from treating philosophical issues
nonreflectively and which in social work can risk the
result of severing practice from its roots in western
philosophy and theology.

On Knowing and Doing Good in Social Work

The kinds of good which are integrally involved in
social work practice have not been systematically studied. Relevant topics include such extensive subjects as
autonomy and freedom, justice, nonmaleficence (doing no
harm) and beneficence (furthering the well being of
others).[11] There is need to examine these and related
concepts in terms of day to day professional practice.

111

The recent attention focused upon the new social work code of ethics has in fact stimulated an increasing recognition of the need for more knowledge in this area.[12]

Beneficence particularly needs to be reflected upon because it includes questions about what is good for whom and who decides--crucial questions in social work practice. Concomitantly there is also a need to analyze what is meant by evil--another difficult word for social workers. If pressed, social workers would have to admit the presence of the maleficent--the abhorent, the destructive--although such concepts are notably absent in social work theory and literature. Social workers are more acquainted with meaninglessness which can often be seen as a despair rooted in a loss of belief in the possibility of good--or even the possibility of knowledge of the good.

In concepts of good and evil the social nature of the self is again evident. Evil can be described as that which is destructive of selves. To take an extreme example, knowledge of the Holocaust cannot be escaped. It occurred in this century in a world characterized by modern technology, and it sought the destruction of humanity--in its victims and unknowingly also in its perpetrators.[13]

Polanyi and Prosch refer to the "blind moral passions" seen first in Marxism and later in the Nazis, which resulted from the growth of a technological society in which a belief in materialism and science led to an abrogation of traditional moral values. The result was the exercise of naked power and the use of violence unrestrained by moral principles. They say:

> In such men the traditional forms for holding
> moral ideals had been shattered and their moral
> passions diverted into the only channels which
> a strictly mechanistic conception of man and
> society left open to them. We may describe
> this as a process of moral inversion. The
> morally inverted person has not merely perform-
> ed a philosophic substitution of material pur-
> poses for moral aims; he is acting with the
> whole force of his homeless moral passions
> within a purely materialistic framework of pur-
> poses. (Second underlining added.)[14]

And Bronowski, who lost many members of his family at Auschwitz, says in his chapter on the uncertainties in all knowledge:

We have to cure ourselves of the itch for absolute knowledge and power. We have to close
the distance between the push-button order and
the human act. We have to touch people.[15]

Touching people in some of the ways Bronowski means is
part of the moral purpose of social work and is related
to the concept of caring discussed in the next chapter.

One of the reasons social workers do not feel comfortable about discussing problems of evil is the basic
concept of nonjudgmentalism which permeates all social
work teaching. This is another concept which needs to
be studied in greater depth. It does not mean that
social workers do not take a position about what is good
and what is not. Basically it means that social workers
do not condemn, or sit in judgment on, other human
beings who come to them for help. The British philosopher R. F. Stalley addressed this issue and concluded
that the emphasis in the field is basically against the
potential of certain negative attitudes or "faults" on
the part of the social worker. The faults to be avoided include authoritarianism or dogmatism with the connotations of coercion, stereotyping, and concern with
punishment for wrong doing.[16]

How dangerous or illegal behavior is dealt with by
social workers is one of the areas which needs to be
studied. A worker may fail both the person and society
in not recognizing and dealing with these issues when
they arise. Ethical issues like these need more attention than they have received in the literature.[17]

Many of the ways in which social work is concerned
with knowing and doing that which is good have yet to
be explored from a philosophical perspective. Here relationship and caring are discussed as illustrative of
the way in which philosophical reflection can further
understanding of the good to be found in social work
practice. In the following discussion an effort will be
made to show that an underlying assumption in practice
is that goodness is caring--caring for persons, for
other selves.

Robert Morris has addressed the issue of caring in
social work from a somewhat different perspective.[18] He
suggests that the traditional aspect of caring about the
sick, and those vulnerable in other ways, be implemented
by social workers providing more of the direct care-
taking services, including the sponsorship and management of these services. It is not the institutional

structures within which social work operates that is of
concern here, however. The purpose here is to examine
caring in social work practice in the light of its
philosophical meaning and purpose.

On Caring

Caring means that other persons matter, that what
happens makes a difference not only to the person directly affected but also to the others who care. Caring
also provides the motivation to help. From the side of
the person being cared about it often makes the acceptance of help possible because it affirms one's humanity in having worth and corroborates the sense of be-
longing in the world. The earlier discussion of relationship concluded with reference to the integral
connection between relationship and caring, which for
the client "affirm his personal worth and social link-
age," as Perlman says. To a large extent growing up
human is made possible by caring relationships.

In a philosophical treatise written specifically
on caring Mayeroff discusses two related aspects of
caring. The first is caring about persons and wanting
to help particular persons grow and become themselves
in terms of their unique potentialities. The other
aspect deals with caring about things, which in
Mayeroff's sense means primarily ideas and values,
which often require the activity and involvement of that
person to bring them to fruition.

Mayeroff emphasizes how in caring relationships one
desires and seeks the growth of the other in ways which
encourage the uniqueness of that particular other. This
uniqueness, however, is itself embedded in caring relationships. He says:

> To help another person grow is at least to help
> him to care for something or someone apart from
> himself, and it involves encouraging and assist-
> ing him to find and create areas of his own in
> which he is able to care. Also, it is to help
> that other person to come to care for himself,
> and by becoming responsive to his own need to
> care to become responsible for his own life.[19]

Mayeroff acknowledges the contributions Buber has
made to his thought and this is evident in the relevance
to the discussion of such passages in Buber as the following in which the primordial nature of relationship
is elaborated.

The development of the soul in the child is inextricably bound up with that of the longing for the Thou, with the satisfaction and the disappointment of this longing, with the game of his experiments and the tragic seriousness of his perplexity. Genuine understanding of this phenomenon, which is injured by every attempt to lead it back into more confined spheres, can only be promoted if, during its observation and discussion, its cosmic and meta-cosmic origin is kept in mind. For it reaches out from the undivided primal world which precedes form, out of which the bodily individual who is born into the world, but not yet the personal, actualized being, has fully emerged. For only gradually, by entering into relations, is the latter to develop out of this primal world.[20]

The discussion in Mayeroff of the ways caring relationships further growth is relevant to social work and other helping professions. For example, in a related article he says:

Caring involves a rhythm of intervention and receptiveness on our part. These ways of relating are not mutually exclusive; for intervention is also receptive in being responsive and receptivity is in no way detached passivity.[21]

The limitations of such social work methods as the task centered approach of Reid and the recommended procedures of Fischer discussed earlier become apparent when they are seen in the light of the meaning of caring relationships. Caring means wanting the growth of the other and seeking ways of relating which will encourage and foster that growth. It means helping the other to order his life in ways which will help that particular person come to feel at home in his world. Premature doing (e.g., not giving enough time and attentiveness) and the recommending of particular actions may in fact violate that process. Tasks and other techniques can be useful, but when they are the primary emphasis, the person may remain incapacitated in his relationships. If the request for help carried--as many do--an implicit, or even an explicit, plea for help in caring, in the need to be cared about and the need to be helped to be able to care, it will have gone unheard.

It is important that the methods which are taught for the practice of social work be congruent with the underlying values of the profession. Caring, as Mayeroff says, allows one to order and give meaning to one's life, to be at home in the world. Caring also enables one to decide, to _know_, what is valuable. The way in which caring is basic for social work now becomes clearer.

The last section concluded with the suggestion that an implicit assumption in social work is that goodness is caring. It is now possible to argue further for this position. If goodness is what furthers the self's ability to care for itself for its own sake, and for the selves of others for their own sakes, then it would seem clear that a basic presupposition in social work is that goodness is caring. What damages or destroys selves in their ability to care is bad, or even evil. What supports, enhances or augments the ability of an individual to care for himself and for others is good. Whatever else goodness may be in social work practice it must at least be this.

Probing in Socratic fashion to find the underlying assumptions in the actual activity of social workers would in all probability lead to a recognition that, whatever else may also be considered to be good, caring is included in what social work practitioners mean by goodness; caring is what motivates and guides their activities. Evidence for the truth of the statement-- Goodness is caring--is found when what goodness _means_ is found, i.e., when the ability of the person to care for himself for his own sake, and for others for theirs, is found.

It becomes clear then that the statement:

Goodness is caring

is _true_ for social work. It is more than an expression of approval or preference, which is all that is permitted by positivist definitions. It is rather an assertion of a truth that can be _known_, that goodness is caring, an assertion that establishes one of the foundations, possibly the primary one, of ethical behavior in social work practice.

Footnotes

[1] Reamer, "Ethical Content in Social Work," p. 534.

[2] Reamer, "Fundamental Ethical Issues in Social Work," pp. 232-233.

[3] See Cassell, "How Does Interdisciplinary Work?" and Corinna Delkeskamp, "Interdisciplinarity: A Critical Appraisal," in Knowledge, Values and Belief, eds. H. Tristram Engelhardt, Jr. and Daniel Callahan (Hastings-on-Hudson, New York: The Hastings Center, 1977), pp. 324-354.

[4] Reamer, "Fundamental Ethical Issues in Social Work," p. 242.

[5] Ibid.

[6] F. E. McDermott, ed., Self Determination in Social Work (London: Routledge & Kegan Paul, 1975).

[7] Raymond Plant, Social and Moral Theory in Casework (London: Routledge & Kegan Paul, 1970), p. 90.

[8] Bill Jordan, Helping in Social Work (London: Routledge & Kegan Paul, 1979), p. 132.

[9] Cassell, "How Does Interdisciplinary Work?", p. 359.

[10] Ibid., pp. 360-61.

[11] This listing is adapted from Tom L. Beauchamp and James F. Childress, Principles of Biomedical Ethics (New York: Oxford University Press, 1979).

[12] See, for example, Reamer and Abramson, The Teaching of Social Work Ethics and Loewenberg and Dolgoff, Ethical Decisions for Social Work Practice.

[13] See Philip Hallie, "From Cruelty to Goodness," The Hastings Center Report 11 (June 1981):23-28.

[14] Polanyi and Prosch, _Meaning_, p. 18.

[15] Bronowski, _Ascent of Man_, p. 374.

[16] R. F. Stalley, "Non-judgmental Attitudes," in _Philosophy in Social Work_, eds. Timms and Watson, pp. 95-96.

[17] See David G. Hardman, "Not with my Daughter, You Don't," _Social Work_ 20 (July 1975) :278-285.

[18] Robert Morris, "Caring for vs. Caring about People," _Social Work_, Vol. 22, No. 5 (September 1977).

[19] Milton Mayeroff, _On Caring_ (New York: Harper & Row, 1971; Perennial Library, 1972), pp. 10-11.

[20] Buber, _I and Thou_, p. 28.

[21] Milton Mayeroff, "On Caring," _International Philosophical Quarterly_ V (September 1965) :465.

CHAPTER X

ULTIMATE QUESTIONS AND MEANINGS

Various definitions of the word ultimate indicate that it is used in a variety of ways which push to the outer limits of thought and of human concerns. Definitions include references to that which is the smallest unit or the largest possible, to what is most fundamental and to what is all encompassing, and, most significantly for the discussion here, to what is deemed to be of the greatest importance and to that which is accepted as final and conclusive.[1] It is another word, like moral, and good and evil, which is apt to make social workers uneasy, perhaps because in the early history of social work it seemed to be associated with personal salvation seen as a reward rather than related to real concern for others.[2]

Whatever the history of the word in social work, however, it does refer to a dimension which must be recognized and acknowledged as an integral part of human life. It is there whether or not it is attended to directly. A society, which is predominantly materialistic and bound in its thought, as well as in its physical aspects, to technology and to positivist science, will try to view such concerns as problems to be solved, if not now then later. One extreme example of this kind of effort to evade the issues is the attempt to use cryogenics to thwart death.

When philosophical thought pushes far enough it eventually confronts the basic question of _why_ anything is. It is the question which lies beyond efforts to understand and define _what_ is and includes the integrally related inquiry into how human beings can know what is.

Mystery in Human Life

Most ultimate questions are, ultimately, mysteries, another word in disrepute in modern society. A sense of mystery is set against the positivist dictum that what cannot be known, i.e., verified and in a sense possessed, is meaningless. Mystery, like relation is primordial. It includes a sense of wonder--a letting go of the effort to try and manipulate and manage, and permitting oneself to marvel at the world, at being in the world. There are some writers who attribute various current problems in society to a loss of this capacity to wonder. Mystery is difficult to discuss because to

119

a large extent it is beyond words which confine without the ability to define. Words like dread and awe (even awful) and tragic are relevant in that they express both amazement and the kind of fearfulness humans experience when aware of this dimension of life which cannot be truly described and is experienced as beyond human control.

Hubris, scientific or professional, can lead to a denial of mystery. In positivist terms what cannot be confined in empirical definitions and verified by sense data can be consigned to the meaningless. The result is a world experienced as barren of meaning--as silent and indifferent, at times even malignant--in the face of ultimate questions like why is there life and why is there my life, why is there caring and relation-- and what of reverence and all that it connotes.

Mystery cannot be discussed as content, only as a dimension of human life. The difficulties of language can be avoided by remaining silent. Wittgenstein utilized this approach when writing the _Tractatus_, a book on logic useful to his positivist successors. According to Barrett, in writing to his publisher Wittgenstein indicated that the most important part of his book was what he did not say. Barrett says:

> The place of 'the mystical' is identified quite
> simply and tersely: '_That_ the world is, is the
> mystical.' Science tells us _how_ the world is;
> it describes the myriad kinds of phenomena,
> their behavior, and their mutual interactions
> one with another. But before the sheer fact
> of the world's existence, _that_ there is a world
> at all, that anything at all exists, in Leibniz's
> telling phrase, we can only stand in silent awe.
> Before this primal mystery of Being our human
> chatter falters. Here language can only point,
> and then pass into silence. 'Of that whereof
> we cannot speak we must be silent.'[3]

The difficulty with remaining silent, however, is that there is even more room for misinterpretation than in using words to try to describe what cannot be described. For this reason, despite the difficulties, it is important to make an effort to discuss this dimension of human life.

Thinking about mystery requires an awareness of being. At this point in this discussion it is argued that the nature of knowing as relevant to social work is integrally related to the nature of being, and that, as Marcel says, being is prior to knowing, and is the only context in which knowing takes place. He says:

> From this standpoint, contrary to what epistemology seeks vainly to establish, there exists well and truly a mystery of cognition; knowledge is contingent on a participation in being for which no epistemology can account because it continually presupposes it.[4]

Marcel's further discussions of the mystery of being are enlightening here. With reference to the human effort to reflect on one's reflections, to think oneself, as he would say, a difference in attitude from that of problem solving can be seen. Of such problem solving he says:

> In such a case I work on the data, but everything leads me to believe that I need not take into account the I who is at work--it is a factor which is presupposed and nothing more.[5]

He continues:

> Here, on the contrary, what I would call the ontological status of the investigator assumes a decisive importance. Yet so long as I am concerned with thought itself I seem to follow an endless regression. But by the very fact of recognizing it as endless I transcend it in a certain way: I see that this process takes place within an affirmation of being--an affirmation which I am rather than an affirmation which I utter: by uttering it I break it, I divide it, I am on the point of betraying it.[6]

This is the context in which Marcel stresses that being is prior to knowledge, that being is not explained by, is not reducible to, the content of what is known. Being is characterized by presence, not by data.

It is important to emphasize that for Marcel those matters which are problems are in principle soluble; various techniques are available or can be found. Mystery refers to those questions for which there are no answers--which cannot be answered because there is no way even to frame the question without becoming entangled and interfering with the conditions of the answer and thus begging the question. The answer is pre-

supposed in the question. Mysteries include the ultimate questions: Why is there a world rather than nothing? Did the world have a beginning in time? Is there
an Author, Creator of the world? Presence is also a
mystery. There is no way to experience presence, or to
define it, without being involved in it--it can only be
known from the inside, it cannot be grasped from the
outside.

> A problem is something which I meet, which I
> find complete before me, but which I can
> therefore lay siege to and reduce. But a
> mystery is something in which I myself am in-
> volved, and it can therefore only be thought
> of as 'a sphere where the distinction between
> what is in me and what is before me loses its
> meaning and its initial validity.'[7]

One of the ways Marcel illustrates what he means
by presence is the difference experienced in relationship to the person who is really present, who is available, one might even say whose being is attentive, and
the person who is there physically but not really present, and hence in an important sense is unavailable.
He describes the latter situation as communication without communion.

> He understands what I say to him, but he does
> not understand me: I may even have the ex-
> tremely disagreeable feeling that my own words,
> as he repeats them to me, as he reflects them
> back at me, have become unrecognizable. By a
> very singular phenomenon indeed, this stranger
> interposes himself between me and my own reality,
> he makes me in some sense also a stranger to my-
> self; I am not really myself when I am with him.[8]

In contrast, he says:

> When somebody's presence does really make it-
> self felt, it can refresh my inner being; it
> reveals me to myself, it makes me more fully
> myself than I should be if I were not exposed
> to its impact.[9]

While surely presence is much to be desired in a
social worker, Marcel points out the difficulties, sometimes even the absurdities, in trying to teach someone
how to be present. In social work it would seem to be
associated with a will, desire, wish to be present to
another so as to help, enhance, support that person.

This wish and this capacity is often what prospective
social workers bring to their learning efforts. This
quality of being capable of presence needs to be fostered, nurtured, encouraged. It can be seen to be in jeop-
ardy in an educational program which concentrates on
techniques and manipulations.

Another area which can be endangered by the failure
to recognize the importance of presence is in situations
characterized by special vulnerabilities, which in some
cultures assures those thus exposed of care and pro-
tection. Marcel uses the examples of a sleeping child
and of guests who may be defenseless in a variety of
ways and who traditionally in many societies are wel-
comed and protected for just this reason. Marcel says,
"This sacredness of the unprotected lies at the roots
of what we might call a metaphysics of hospitality."[10]
Regarding western society he says:

> The more, it might be said, the ideas of effi-
> ciency and output assert their supreme author-
> ity, the more this attitude of reverence to-
> wards the guest, towards the wounded, towards
> the sick, will appear at first incomprehensible,
> and later absurd: and in fact, in the world
> around us, we know that this assertion of the
> absurdity of forbearance and generosity is tak-
> ing very practical shapes.[11]

The work from which this was taken was published in
Great Britain in 1950 and could be seen as prophetic in
terms of trends in the United States in the 1980's.

Basic to Marcel's thought also is man's communal
nature. He addresses the same issue present in Buber's
I-Thou.

> Two things seem to me to be of importance.
> First, we must understand that this enquiry can
> be developed only if we take a certain fullness
> of life as our starting point; secondly, we
> must at the same time note well that this full-
> ness of life can in no circumstances be that
> of my own personal experience considered in an
> exclusively private aspect, considered inasmuch
> as it is just mine; rather must it be that of a
> whole which is implied by the relation to the
> with, by the togetherness, on which last year
> I laid such emphasis.

. . .

But to take up such a position immediately throws into relief the essentially anti-cartesian character of the metaphysic to which we shall have to direct ourselves. It is not enough to say that it is a metaphysic of being; it is a metaphysic of we are as opposed to a metaphysic of I think.[12]

From the standpoint of relevance to social work it is also important to note Marcel's sense that the philosophical effort to understand oneself leads to a greater understanding of others. The more acute the perception of one's own being, the greater is one's capacity to understand the experience of others.[13]

Implicit in Marcel's assertion of the essential mystery of being is the recognition that only thus is it possible to understand the dimensions of what it means to be fully human. If this dimension is ruled out of bounds in terms of what social workers can seek to know and to understand, much of what is human will be eliminated from consideration and to that extent the persons concerned will be diminished.

Human beings by virtue of being human do become involved in mystery and in ultimate questions. An inquiry into this involvement requires the language and imagery of art and participation in the reasoning and insights of some of the other explorers called philosophers and theologians.

Life and Death Issues

It is often the impact of death which brings ultimate questions to the fore--either the prospect of one's own death or the loss of another. Death seems to break in on life although in fact its potential is ever present. To some degree all human beings know at some level, often through experiences of separation starting early in life, that they will die, and the effort to avoid this knowledge becomes more difficult with the passage of time. A recent reviewer comments about a book by Malcolm Cowley at age 80:

> One question stretches through it: What can be done in the time remaining? Of course it is the only question ever, whatever our ages.[14]

Part of the difficulty for the individual, but also for society, is that for the most part no one knows how much time does remain.

The evidence of the effort to evade the knowledge of the inevitability of death are abundant in modern society. Examples can be seen in funeral practices which seek to somehow disguise the evidence that life has truly gone and which suggest that meaning can be found through efforts to forestall the final dissolution of the physical body. Psychoanalysts have sometimes participated in the denial of the meaning of death by interpreting the fear of death as basically a fear of castration.[15]

On the other hand, however, there are societal trends which emphasize the need of the dying to be ministered to--not just by the clergy, but by all who come in contact with them. There is a proliferation of academic courses on death and dying and an increasing understanding of the processes of mourning. There is also notably a growing recognition that the failure to mourn, to truly experience the depths of feeling associated with loss, can damn up the life forces in a person so that loving and caring may no longer be possible for that person until the grief has been truly experienced and finally accepted--sometimes after a lapse of years.

The threat of death, the experience of dying, and the sometimes shattering experience of loss, are times in life when caring is vital. The human need for caring others is omnipresent but can be seen to be most acute at these times. Earlier the goodness of caring and the importance of relationship were discussed. In addition, reference has been made to the primordial aspect of Buber's I-Thou, Marcel's we are, and Niebuhr's self which "not only knows itself in relation to other selves but exists as self only in that relation." It is apparent then that life is lived in relation to others, that humans are ontologically bound to each other. In this context the way in which people experience death becomes clearer. Loss is an amputation in which the self is in truth diminished and its integrity threatened. Healing takes place through mourning, and finally through the reclamation and the reestablishment of human relationships. There is no short cut. When one's center of gravity has been dislocated everything is disarranged until a new balance is established.

It is clear that if a social worker is to have the capacity to help another, that social worker must be able to face death and what it represents and still be able to affirm life. Being is known in the face of nonbeing. As the Book of Common Prayer says, "In the midst of life we are in death." And even in a materialistic society, "We brought nothing into the world and it is certain we can carry nothing out."

What of death then? It is a mystery. There is mystery in the knowledge of the death of others--in the dramatic contrast between the presence and the absence of life. There is mystery also in the knowledge of one's own death, but this is experienced somewhat differently. One's intrinsic involvement in living means that one's own death is not really believed; this is because of the intractable difficulty of really understanding one's own nonexistence from a position inside existence, which is the only position available to anyone. The mystery of being is also the mystery of non-being.

Existentialism and the Existentialist Theologians

Throughout this discussion there has been an emphasis upon the inadequacies of positivism as a philosophy for social work. It is now suggested that a philosophical position drawing upon the thought of the existentialists holds the potential of providing a more adequate framework for understanding the human activity of social work.

Existentialism is a term used in various ways to apply to a variety of thinkers, many of whom would not accept the word as applicable because it is often used as a label and thus becomes an effort to contain, or encapsulate, thought--a state of affairs ironically diametrically opposed to the emphases in existential thinking. In his recent book, Existential Social Work, Krill lists some of those thinkers who are often called existentialists and who might very well reject the term.16 Krill's book is an effort to apply the concept of existentialism to social work practice. Unfortunately, however, the kind of nomenclature selected results in the abstract concepts being discussed seeming to be confined to specific categories.

For the discussion here no effort will be made to elaborate the ways existentialism might influence specifically what is done in social work practice. Instead the argument will seek to emphasize the point that existentialism represents a way, or even various ways, of looking at human existence from inside--the only ways in fact that it can be looked at, whether this is acknowledged or not. This inside view so to speak will have ramifications in terms of the basic orientation toward that which is human, which is of course that with which social work is concerned.

Despite the variety of ways the word existential is used, it generally represents a philosophical position in which being, living and participating in the world, takes precedence over efforts to reason apart from experience. It arose in this century in a world which had experienced two world wars, the Holocaust, and the advent of the previously unthinkable possibilities of atomic destruction.

Such a world experienced a profound loss in the ability to view life optimistically in terms of rationality and social progress. Often through scientific discoveries the religious thought of previous centuries had also been exposed to profound questioning and skepticism, which, while not new, had certainly become more influential. This loss in the western world of a traditional religious perspective on life combined with the advances in science and technology resulted in a pervasive sense of alienation, of homelessness in the world. It was this situation which was addressed in various ways by those whose work has been called existentialist.

It was also this world in which social work had its origins. As suggested throughout this discussion social work as a human enterprise has been pushed and pulled by these and other historical currents. The effort to adhere to a positivist approach in the profession might be seen to be both a reflection of these issues in the culture and an effort to find something to hold onto. The need to hold on in this way, however, is constricting and unduly limiting. An interesting analogy out of personal experience is suggested by an anecdote provided by the physicist Bohm.

He describes an incident in his childhood in which as a young boy he was confronted with the need to cross a stream by jumping from one rock to another. He found himself paralyzed with anxiety when he stood still and sought to carefully plan his approach to the problem. With a sudden insight he was able to let go of his effort to solve the problem by reasoning and to participate in the experience very differently.

> Suddenly in the middle of the stream I had a
> flash of insight that what I _am_ is to be in
> the state of movement from one rock to the
> next, and that as long as I do not try to map
> out what I will do, I can cross safely, but
> that if I try to proceed from such a map, I
> will fall. Just in that very moment of being

127

on the rock, there was a sudden change in the
whole attitude of my body, along with all my
thinking and feeling on the subject, which not
only immediately removed difficulties with
crossing the streams on rocks, but also affected my whole life thereafter, in many other ways.
For example, since then, a great deal of my work
has been directed toward the understanding of
movement, with the aid of this particular insight, that is, that undivided flowing movement
is what is primary, while its 'map' in thought
is merely an abstraction of distinct 'markers'
that indicate certain salient features of the
movement (as musical ratio is similarly a set
of markers indicating certain salient features
of the movement of the music).17

This analogy has relevance for social work practice also. A kind of flowing movement is characteristic
of a social work interview where an effort is being made
to respond to the person who is in need of help of some
kind. It is difficult for students, and sometimes also
for more experienced workers, to accept that responses,
just because they are responses to another person, cannot be determined beforehand--even though the general
goal or purpose of the interview, i.e., a kind of map,
has been decided upon in advance. The social work process has something of the characteristic Buber refers
to when he speaks of "decision in the depths of spon-
taneity, unruffled decision, made ever anew to right
action." Buber continues:

Then action is not empty, but purposive, en-
joined, needed, part of creation; but this
action is no longer imposed upon the world,
it grows on it as if it were non-action.18

This situation might be described as a full, active
participation in the existential moment and it suggests
the relevance of existential thought to social work
practice.

It is difficult to discuss existentialism in any
summary fashion, but an effort will be made to identify
some of the ideas having particular relevance for the
issues of knowing in social work which are raised here.

The break with the rationalist tradition in philosophy comes about with the assertion that existence precedes essence. This is at times an elusive differentia-
tion in ordinary life as existence and essence are in-

tegrally related in human life. However, the different
emphasis in philosophical thought has ramifications in
terms of how human life is viewed. Barrett says, "The
essence of a thing is <u>what</u> the thing is; existence refers to the sheer fact <u>that</u> the thing is."[19]

When thought tries to reason from essence, it is
possible to forget that such reasoning takes place within the hidden presupposition of being. It was the
nature of this being that the existentialists sought to
elaborate. For some, existentialism became an assertion of being in the face of a world in which traditional meanings were no longer tenable. In such a world
man asserted himself defiantly, as being, as free, despite a contingent world, indifferent at best and hos-
tile at worst.

Ironically, however, the theologian, Kierkegaard,
is generally considered to have been the first to assert
what later came to be called existentialism. Out of
his own intense personal struggles Kierkegaard emphasized the primary importance of the inner man, the subjective inmost feelings including those of fear and
trembling, of dread and desolation, as well as affirmation, without which religion was composed of dry dogma,
leading to arrogance in those who professed to be in
possession of religious truth. It was the assertion of
the vital necessity of inner experience which was
Kierkegaard's primary contribution in the context of the
discussion here. What was to Kierkegaard a revolt
against rationalism also has relevance to the concept of
intellectualization in psychoanalytic terms whereby
something known only intellectually is not really known
because of its separation from the integral and vital
inner feelings.[20]

In terms of elaborating a specific philosophy, existential in nature, Heidegger is most frequently cited.
His philosophy is very complex and too extensive for
any definitive treatment here. At this point, it is
only suggested that his concept of man as being-in-the-
world is a potential source of insight for an expanded
and more adequate philosophical framework for social
work. Concepts of anxiety and dread and efforts to
elaborate the human meanings of estrangement, authenti-
city and solicitude can be seen to be of particular
relevance. Heidegger was not a theologian and eschewed
specific consideration of religious concerns. In fact,
Barrett concludes a recent discussion of the relevance
of his work to the modern world by commenting "<u>Dasein</u>
(the word Heidegger uses for human being) has no soul."[21]

Heidegger's _Dasein_ is not intended to refer to any specific individual but is general in its references, offering only possibilities. Despite this, however, identifying an emptiness at the center of Heidegger's thought, Barrett experiences this suddenly as an insight, or perhaps an intuition, and subsequently seeks to explain it. What is missing seems to be a basic sense of moral commitment. Heidegger brings new understanding to how human beings are in the world, but, Barrett says:

> Our era is the night of the world, Heidegger
> mournfully echoes Holderin, when the old gods
> have fled but the new god has not yet arrived.[22]

The lack seems to be that of a framework for moral commitment--a framework found in the Hebraic--Christian tradition where God is not a philosophic concept and is not therefore subject to being dismissed and abandoned as no longer believable or usable. One has the impression that Heidegger approached the threshold of openness to the possibility of such a God but did not step across.

Ideas from some other philosophers who are existential in their approach and who are also theologians have been mentioned at various points in this discussion. References have been cited from Buber, Marcel, and H. R. Niebuhr. In addition, the work of Paul Tillich should also be mentioned as having particular relevance to the kinds of human activity involved in social work.

Tillich's concept of the courage to be, elaborated in the book by that title, discusses the necessity of accepting the finite condition of being human, and recognizing that at best human knowledge is only partial and may even be mistaken.[23] The courage to be involves the affirmation of life in spite of the existential anxiety associated with non-being which is inevitable because it is rooted in man's finitude. Life is lived and affirmed in spite of non-being, not in an effort to escape awareness of this aspect of human existence.

The philosopher-theologians mentioned above all share a basic orientation to God as the ultimate source of being and of meaning in human life. Their methods are different and they all draw their strength from their own existential situations. Throughout their thought there is an implicit, sometimes also an explicit, recognition that each is who he is individually, per-

sonally free in many ways, but also profoundly conditioned by the specific world into which he was born.

It is the acknowledged religious dimension in their
writing which distinguishes them from philosophers who
are not also theologians.   The existential awareness
of being in the world combined with a religious commitment centers these men both personally and in their
written thoughts.

In their work can be seen how it is possible for
the modern mind to experience religion as freeing
thought, rather than confining it intellectually in
various dogmas, which by their nature require a response
either of acquiescence or revolt.   Instead, being is
seen as related to a creative source of being, and finite man, in recognizing and really experiencing his
finitude, becomes more cautious in asserting the fi-
nality of what he thinks he is able to know.   Being is,
we are, and in this context the courage to be is pos-
sible--the courage to be as finite human beings intrinsically related to each other, grounded in existence
as known and open to the possibility of knowing more--
sometimes in ways different from the familiar, culturally conditioned channels in which most thought takes
place.

Footnotes

[1] See, for example, The American Heritage Dictionary of the English Language, 1969 ed., s.v. ultimate.

[2] Mary Richmond referred to this motivation when
she said: "The spirit of the mediaeval church, too,
encouraged charitable giving in the main 'as a species
of fire insurance.'   The poor, when they were thought of
at all, were too likely to be regarded as a means of
saving the giver's soul."   (Friendly Visiting Among the
Poor, p. 4).

[3] Barrett, Illusion of Technique, pp. 51-52.

[4] Gabriel Marcel, "On the Ontological Mystery," in
Philosophy in the Twentieth Century, eds. Barrett and
Aiken, 2:370.

[5] Ibid., p. 369.

[6] Ibid.

[7] Gabriel Marcel, Mystery of Being, vol. 1: Reflection and Mystery; vol. 2: Faith and Reality (Great Britain: Harvill Press, 1950; Gateway Edition, 1960), 2:211.

[8] Ibid., 1:205.

[9] Ibid.

[10] Ibid., 1:217.

[11] Ibid.

[12] Ibid., 2:9-10.

[13] Ibid., 2:7.

[14] Donald Hall, review of The View from 80, by Malcolm Cowley, in The New York Times Book Review, 7 September 1980, p. 15.

[15] See discussion in Theodore Lidz, The Person, rev. ed. (New York: Basic Books, 1976), p. 535.

[16] Donald F. Krill, Existential Social Work (New York: Free Press, 1978), p. 22.

[17] David Bohm, "Insight, Knowledge, Science and Human Values," Teachers College Record 82 (Spring 1981), p. 391.

[18] Buber, I and Thou, p. 109.

[19] William Barrett, Irrational Man, A Study in Existential Philosophy (Garden City, New York: Doubleday, 1958; Doubleday Anchor Books, 1962), p. 102.

[20]Bruce Wilshire, "Kierkegaard's Theory of Knowledge and New Directions in Psychology and Psychoanalysis," Review of Existential Psychology and Psychiatry III (Fall 1963):256.

[21]Barrett, Illusion of Technique, p. 234.

[22]Ibid., p. 244.

[23]Paul Tillich, The Courage to Be (New Haven: Yale
University Press, 1952).

CHAPTER XI

SUMMARY AND RECOMMENDATIONS

Throughout its history two themes can be seen to have been consistently emphasized in social work. Humanitarian concerns have always been integrally involved in the profession. In addition, the importance of knowledge, primarily scientific knowledge, has been continuously stressed. These two themes, both related to questions about what can be known and how it is known, tend to be poorly integrated. Students, educators, and practitioners are all expected to subscribe to specified humanitarian values, which are nevertheless seen as basically preferences, and hence without real cognitive status in an academic world in which the tendency is to consider knowledge to be only that which is scientific. In addition, the traditional emphasis upon art in the practice of social work is at times treated apologetically, occasionally even with the suggestion that this aspect of practice represents only a temporary state of affairs until social work can become truly scientific. The lack of integration of these two themes, scientific knowledge and human values, is seen here to be the result of a positivist definition of knowledge which has been accepted in an unexamined way by academic social work, as well as by society at large including the broader academic community.

The situation is described in an educational journal.

> There has arisen in the modern world an increasingly dominant view that we can know only that which we can count, measure, and weigh. In this view--and it often dominates modern education in the schools and in the media-feeling, imagination, the will, intuitive insight, are regarded as having little or nothing to do with knowledge, and are frequently even disparaged as sources of irrationality. In this view of knowledge and knowing there is no place for purpose, mind, meaning, and values as constituent of reality. Humanist educational reforms have time and again foundered on failure to engage the issue of what counts as genuine knowledge about the world. Indeed humanists have often been enthusiastic collaborators in their own undoing, at one moment seeking to out-science the scientists, and at the next acquiescing in the view that they deal only

with inspiring and entertaining fancies. In consequence our conceptions of knowledge often give rise to views of the world that provide little support for human values and for an education in which persons and the values of persons remain central.[1]

This narrow positivistic definition of what constitutes knowledge can have particularly serious repercussions in social work practice, which is essentially a person to person activity requiring knowledge of what it means to be human. This discussion identifies the historical roots of the positivist definition of knowledge in modern society and explicates ways in which this definition can be seen to be particularly inadequate for social work.

The primary thrust of the discussion is to call attention to the ways the assumptions of positivism have often unwittingly been incorporated into academic approaches to the study of social work, to question these assumptions, and to suggest some possible directions for exploration in the effort to develop a philosophical framework comprehensive enough to encompass and integrate the various kinds of knowledge needed for this human and humane activity.

The roots of positivism have been seen to be in the dualism of Descartes who lived during the seventeenth century. Descartes, reasoning on the basis of belief in a veracious God who would not allow him to be deceived, divided the world into two aspects. One he believed to be the really real, objective, out there aspects which could be known through the methods of mathematical physics, that is, res extensa, the world of shapes, mass, motion, and singleness or plurality. The second was the internal, subjective world, that is, res cogitans, the world of mind, which because it was internal was seen as subject to illusion and basically not to be depended upon to give an accurate picture of the real world.

Subsequently the positivists believed that all that qualified as knowledge were those things which can be known through sense data, manipulated by mathematical techniques, and verified by specific observations. All other aspects of the world, if they existed at all, were to be considered unknowable and/or meaningless. It has been suggested here that the philosophy of positivism has been found wanting in modern physics, the paradigm for positivism. In academic social work, however, the positivist influence has either not been explicitly recognized or has been accepted in an unanalyzed way on the assumption that it, and only it, represents that which is truly scientific.[2]

There are several problems associated with a positivist position which for the most part have not been noted in social work. For example, there are questions about how the intrinsically subjective nature of sense experience can be transmuted into a representation of the posited really real world.

In addition it has not generally been recognized that in positivism there is a problem in relationship to decisions about what is to count as verification. The early positivist dictum--that in order for any concept to be considered meaningful it must be possible to specify what observations would verify it--remains influential in current attitudes in social work research. Note has not been taken in the social work literature of the later modification of the positivist position in which the verification criterion was recognized as basically a recommendation. As a recommendation it can be analyzed from the standpoint of whether or not it is a good recommendation, i.e., it can be seen as a value judgment and studied as such, rather than accepted as representing immutable law. The problem of verification is seen as particularly significant for the discussion here with reference to the way effectiveness is defined and judged in social work practice.

Attention has been called to the rhetoric of some of the positivists in which verbal techniques which denigrate any other approaches to knowledge are utilized. Belittling references are sometimes flagrant, but more often are subtle and capitalize on the way this philosophy has been accepted unconsciously by several generations of students and teachers as a result of its unremitting emphasis in the academic world and in the culture at large. As indicated in the quotation from Polanyi referred to earlier:

> We are born into a language, and we are also
> born into a set of beliefs about the nature
> of things. And, once brought up in our be-
> liefs, we embrace them with sufficient con-
> viction to participate in imposing them on the
> next generation.[3]

The discussion here represents an effort to question some of these beliefs about the nature of things--particularly those related to a positivist definition of what can be considered to be knowledge. Emphasis is upon the intrinsic relationship between the knowing person and what is known. Knowledge is then seen as Heisenberg says as "part of the interplay between nature and ourselves," and as describing "nature as exposed to our method of questioning."[4] All knowledge involves personal participation and is in this sense personal knowledge. Polanyi's concepts of personal knowledge, including the vital contribution of tacit knowing to scientific as well as to other kinds of knowledge is discussed. Tacit knowledge is also seen as enlightening in regard to how various forms of art further human knowing and understanding.

The use of different kinds of language--mathematical, verbal and artistic--is seen as a vital part of being human. Self consciousness and knowledge of limitation and death are discussed as dimensions of human life which require verbal and artistic languages for expression and for whatever understanding is possible for finite beings.

Knowledge is seen as intrinsically related to being, which is considered to be primary. Relationship, as in Buber's I-Thou and Marcel's we are, is seen as primordial and thus integrally related to human life in the only ways humans are able to know it. It is also suggested that this ontological status of relationship makes it possible to know what is good and valuable in human life. It is argued that, whatever else goodness may be additionally, it includes caring which is implicit in social work practice.

Human beings are seen as involved in ultimate concerns, but ultimate knowledge is recognized as always conditioned by finite being. Throughout history mankind has repetitiously succumbed to the temptation to assert conditional knowledge as absolute, and thus to claim certainty and the right to coerce others on this basis. Claims for such certainty are seen here to be the result of hubris and to represent error with reference to aspects of life about which human knowledge cannot be completely certain.

Social workers deal with the various difficulties human beings have in living, in relationships with each other and with their world in all its various aspects. The limited view of positivistic definitions of knowledge leads in the direction of reducing human beings to mechanisms which can then be manipulated by techniques.

The caution quoted from Barrett in the beginning continues throughout this discussion. "The technique cannot produce the philosophy that directs it." A growing emphasis on the use of specific techniques designed to fit positivist criteria raises questions related to the need for congruence with the underlying values and moral commitments of the profession. This emphasis on techniques can be seen as a reversal of direction in which techniques become primary rather than being selected and governed by the underlying philosophy. Aristotle's admonition can be seen to be relevant here:

> It is the mark of the educated man and a proof of his culture that in every subject he looks for only so much precision as its nature permits.[5]

Aspects of social work practice can and must be studied in order to assure that people are served well and their basic humanity affirmed. There is a need for research into social work as it is actually practiced. This kind of study would seek to understand what experienced social workers do and why they do it. The intrinsic involvement of the person of the worker in what is done could then be recognized as an intrinsic part of practice--something which can be studied and understood, not something to be discounted as negative subjectivism. The use of experienced workers is suggested as most likely to lead to an identification of the qualities involved. Students, for example, are for the most part learning what to do, and do not yet understand what they are doing and why they might be doing it. There would therefore be a risk that students would be focussed narrowly on techniques and their observable effects rather than on a multidimensional study of actual practice and its results.

Research methods for this kind of study might be developed which would only minimally interfere with the processes involved. An analogy might be drawn with reference to the work of certain physicists in which it is recognized that some of the most significant processes not only cannot be stopped in order to be studied, but that in fact the researcher disturbs what he is studying and this must be considered in the way the results are interpreted.

If such research efforts into actual practice were seen to be in the nature of a search, an effort to understand, clarify, and ultimately refine social work approaches to human problems, this could be a cooperative effort in which workers themselves would be enlisted to think about their activities and to share their thoughts with those doing the research. The particular perspectives and methods of the researchers might then be able to design methods of study for practice related to what social work is really about. For example, the concept of effectiveness might be expanded to include such human, person to person qualities as those involved in caring about and affirming the selves of those for whom social work exists. With this kind of perspective some research efforts might be refocused to study social work from the standpoint of the basic goods which it is designed to implement. The use of various techniques would then be evaluated in the light of philosophical concepts which give coherence and meaning to human beings and hence to the social work process.

This view of the possibilities of research as a way of understanding more about social work as practiced is not new. It has been recommended by a number of authors at various points in the history of the profession. Bartlett writing in 1964 urged more research into social work practice. She said:

> Therefore, as some writers point out, at this time we probably 'know more than we know we know,'[6] and one of the important tasks in building knowledge will be to extract from the experienced practitioner what has been learned through expert practice.[7]

Hollis also emphasized the importance of insisting "on modifying the (social science) tools to study social work, not social work to fit the tools."[8]

Boehm has called attention to the fact that:

> Social work theorists repeatedly have stated that social work knowledge must be drawn from the phenomenon of practice and that it stems from research into the nature of social work, its goals and functions, the analysis of its professional activities, the tasks it performs, and the processes it uses.[9]

In a recent publication sponsored by the National Association of Social Workers dealing with the question of research and social work practice, the way in which researchers and practitioners are often at loggerheads is noted, and attempts are made to ameliorate the situation by encouraging cooperation between the two.[10]

Some of the obstacles to cooperation are discussed in
this book and in various other articles.[11] Fanshel
notes a point of particular relevance here:

> The issue of effectiveness has perhaps been
> used in a tyrannizing way and overemphasized
> at the expense of research that would illu-
> minate the treatment processes used by practi-
> tioners. Evaluative studies are not the only
> investigations that are useful to the profes-
> sion.[12]

Some authors point out that research into practice is
complex and often not very neat from an empirical
standpoint.[13]

It is suggested here that a major obstacle to the
kind of cooperation being generally advocated is the
underlying positivist assumption that only that which
is scientific qualifies as knowledge. This focus leads
in turn to an emphasis upon the importance of developing a technology--in this case a technology for prac-
tice--an approach which favors methods which are themselves based in technology and define the results in
technological terms. Many examples from the current
literature could be cited. Rothman in recommending
adaptation of the Research and Development (R&D) approach suggests that it is important "to define the
research task as one of engineering rather than traditional knowledge building."[14] Thomas says, "Knowledge
utilization is that process by which knowledge from research is transformed into social technology."[15]

As has been emphasized throughout the discussion
here, technology is essential in the modern world, but
all that is human with which social workers are required
to deal cannot be encompassed in this kind of framework.
In addition, technology can be used for good or for
ill--to support human growth and development or to de-
humanize. Its purposes are directed by a philosophy of
some kind and in modern academic social work that philosophy tends to be positivism. Until this underlying
philosophical position is recognized explicitly and
dealt with openly in an atmosphere hospitable to differing points of view, it can be expected that tensions
between researchers and practitioners originating in
this point of view will continue to inhibit joint efforts at understanding practice.

For practitioners it is important to abjure any
tendency to identify with the aggressor when attacked

in the name of scientific research based upon positivism, and to affirm that what they do is good and needed and could be better if it were further studied and understood. Researchers should be encouraged to participate in a joint effort with practitioners - an effort in which there would be no place for scapegoats and no need, on either side, to try to prove worth at the expense of the other.

The methods associated with what has been called grounded theory might provide a perspective for this kind of effort.[16] Grounded theory building is an approach to qualitative research. It is basically inductive and seeks to bring to the subject being studied the analytic skills of the researcher focused on finding out what is going on, and what is contributing to what is going on, i.e., generating theory from studying the activity rather than designing the activity to fit the theory. The kind of effort needed might be based upon an approach which says to social workers, in effect, let us try to understand what you are doing, your reasons for doing it, and how your activity is experienced by the person of the client.

Admittedly this would be a complex project, but recognizing the complexity might militate against the risks of oversimplification and avoid certain pitfalls, such as changing what is being studied into something else in order to fit the theory being tested overtly or covertly. In addition, it needs to be recognized that a philosophy like positivism limits the nature of the questions which will be asked and therefore also limits what will be perceived. Heisenberg's comment about natural science comprising "nature as exposed to our method of questioning" is relevant here in the sense that questions associated with techniques based upon positivism will reveal only that part of what constitutes practice about which questions have been asked.

Better communication between practitioners and researchers might well mitigate the problem of what Gordon calls "methodologically impeccable research that is unintelligible or irrelevant to practitioners." The purpose of grounded research would be to develop or elaborate theories which inform the techniques of social work as it is, or might be practiced. Such theories, however, also need to be integrated into a philosophy more adequate than positivism to address all the dimensions of human life which from time to time confront the social worker.

Social work needs a philosophy which does justice
to these other dimensions of human life, a philosophy
which recognizes the way truth can be expressed through
the various human languages whereby coherence and meaning for human lives are found. Reason and disciplined
thinking, as well as intuition and insight, characterize
scientific research and also philosophical efforts to
understand what it means to be human.

In addition to research directed toward understanding activities which characterize practice, the
development of a more adequate philosophical framework
for understanding social work requires an inquiry into
the thinking of other philosophers who are not positivists. Such an exploration would entail interdisciplinary efforts between social workers and philosophers in
order to question assumptions taken for granted in the
everyday discourse of a profession. Philosophical concepts are not readily understandable to most social
workers who see their daily activities as dealing with
more mundane matters. It has not been recognized that
failure to attend to underlying philosophical issues
can be detrimental to the profession and hence to the
human beings for whom it exists. If techniques are not
analyzed in the light of an adequate philosophical
framework, they will reflect an unexamined philosophy
operating sub rosa. This is the situation with regard
to positivism which imposes a seemingly simple, narrow
and restricted view on a profession whose raison d'etre
is rooted in the complicated difficulties and confusions
that characterize human life.

There is no specific philosophy which can be seen
to be readily translatable into the context of social
work practice. It is suggested here, however, that because social work is concerned essentially with human
experience, the relevance of some of the existentialists
should be explored in greater depth than has been done
so far. In addition, despite historical struggles between scientists and the institutional church, it is
further suggested that the ideas of those existential
philosophers who are also theologians have potential for
freeing thought and guarding against the human arrogance
which claims certainty and the right to coerce for various humanly constructed theories and world views. All
human knowledge is seen as finite by these thinkers.
Error is introduced by efforts to encapsulate knowledge
and to declare that either the final answers have been
found or that the method for achieving such certainty
has been developed.

Social work requires a broader philosophical framework than that provided by positivism which has been
accepted in an unexamined way, particularly by academic
social work. This discussion constitutes an effort to
call attention to the seriousness and urgency of this
issue. The lack of integration in the emphases upon
knowledge and values as operating on different tracks
in social work is seen as reflective of this failure
to engage the issues at the appropriate philosophical
level. This failure leaves the profession open to the
risks of operating in terms of a reductive, diminished
view of human nature and what can be known about it.
These philosophical problems, which are both old and
new, must be addressed directly rather than by subtle
innuendo and the denigration of differing points of
view. The first step is an "awakening out of acceptance" with a recognition that a profession intrinsically concerned with human beings requires a philosophy
of knowing capable of encompassing all that is human.

Footnotes

[1] Douglas Sloan, Introduction to "Knowledge, Education and Human Values: Toward the Recovery of Wholeness," Teachers College Record 82 (Spring 1981):373-374.

[2] For a detailed discussion of the limitations of
the closely related difficulties associated with logical empiricism as a philosophy of science for research
in social work, the reader is referred to Heineman, "The
Obsolete Scientific Imperative in Social Work Research."

[3] "Scientific Thought and Social Reality," p. 75.

[4] Physics and Philosophy, p. 81.

[5] Aristotle, Nichomachean Ethics, Book I, in Classics
of Western Philosophy, ed. Steven M. Cahn (Indianapolis:
Hackett Publishing, 1977), pp. 116-117.

[6] See the earlier discussion of Polanyi's concept
of the tacit dimension, especially p. 81.

[7] Harriett M. Bartlett, "The Place and use of Knowledge in Social Work Practice," Social Work 9 (July 1964):38.

[8]Florence Hollis, "Contemporary Issues for Case-workers," in Ego-Oriented Casework, eds. Howard J. Parad and Roger R. Miller (New York: Family Service Association of America, 1963), p. 15.

[9]Werner W. Boehm, "Social Work Education: Issues and Problems in Light of Recent Developments," Journal of Education for Social Work 12 (Winter 1976):26.

[10]David Fanshel, ed., Future of Social Work Research (Washington, D.C.: National Association of Social Workers, 1980).

[11]See also Terry Eisenberg Carrilio, "The Impact of Research in a Family Service Agency," Social Casework 62 (February 1981):87-94.

[12]David Fanshel, "The Future of Social Work Research: Strategies for the Coming Years," in Future of Social Work Research, p. 14.

[13]Jack Rothman, "Harnessing Research to Enhance Practice: A Research and Development Model," in Future of Social Work Research, p. 76.

[14]Ibid., p. 83.

[15]Edwin J. Thomas, "Beyond Knowledge Utilization in Generating Human Service Technology," in Future of Social Work Research, p. 95.

[16]See, for example, Barney G. Glaser and Anselm L. Strauss, The Discovery of Grounded Theory, Strategies for Qualitative Research (Chicago: Aldine Publishing, 1967).

Bibliography

The following is a selective bibliography only. It includes some of the important relevant materials which are likely to be the least familiar to social workers in this country. For a more detailed bibliography the reader is referred to the footnotes at the end of each chapter.

Arendt, Hannah. "Thinking and Moral Considerations: A Lecture." Social Research 38 (Autumn 1971):417-446.

Barrett, William. The Illusion of Technique, Garden City, New York: Anchor Press/Doubleday, 1978.

_____. Irrational Man, A Study in Existential Philosophy. Garden City, New York: Doubleday, 1958; Doubleday Anchor Books, 1962.

Barrett, William and Aiken, Henry D., eds. Philosophy in The Twentieth Century, 2 Vols., New York: Random House, 1962.

Bohm, David. "Insight, Knowledge, Science and Human Values," Teachers College Record 82 (Spring 1981): 380-402.

_____. "On Insight and Its Significance for Science, Education, and Values." Teachers College Record 80 (February 1979):404-419.

Bronowski, J. The Ascent of Man. Boston: Little Brown, 1973.

Broudy, Harry S. "Tacit Knowing as a Rationale for Liberal Education." In Education and Values, pp. 50-66. Edited by Douglas Sloan. New York: Teachers College Press, 1980.

Buber, Martin. Between Man and Man. Translated by Ronald Gregor Smith. Boston: Beacon Press, 1955.

_____. The Knowledge of Man. Edited with an Introduction by Maurice Friedman. New York: Harper & Row, 1965.

Butrym, Zofia T. The Nature of Social Work. London: Macmillan Press, Ltd., 1976.

147

Cassell, Eric J. "How Does Interdisciplinary Work Get Done?" In Knowledge, Value and Belief, pp. 355-361. Edited by H. Tristram Englehardt, Jr. and Daniel Callahan. Hastings-on-Hudson, New York: The Hastings Center, 1977.

Cousins, Norman. Anatomy of an Illness as Perceived by the Patient. New York: W. W. Norton, 1979, Bantam Books, 1981.

Gallagher, Kenneth T. The Philosophy of Knowledge. New York: Sheed and Ward, 1964.

Gouldner, Alvin W. "Anti-Minotaur: The Myth of a Value-Free Sociology." Social Problems 9 (1962): 201-214.

Hallie, Philip. "From Cruelty to Goodness," The Hastings Center Report 11 (June 1981):23-28.

Heineman, Martha Brunswick. "The Obsolete Scientific Imperative in SocialWork Research." Social Service Review 55 (September 1981):371-397.

Heisenberg, Werner. Physics and Philosophy. New York: Harper & Brothers, 1958; Harper Torchbooks, 1962.

Hempel, Carl G. "Problems and Changes in the Empiricist Criterion of Meaning." In Philosophical Problems of Science and Technology, pp. 301-320. Edited by Alex C. Michalos. Boston: Allyn & Bacon, 1974.

Holton, Gerald. Thematic Origins of Scientific Thought: Kepler to Einstein. Cambridge, Massachusetts: Harvard University Press, 1973.

Marcel, Gabriel. The Mystery of Being. Vol. 1: Reflection and Mystery. Great Britain: Harvil Press, 1950; Gateway Editions, 1960.

_____. The Mystery of Being. Vol. 2: Faith and Reality. Great Britain: Harvill Press, 1951; Gateway Edition, 1960.

_____. "On the Ontological Mystery." In Philosophy in the Twentieth Century, Vol. 2, pp. 364-386. Edited by William Barrett and Henry D. Aiken. New York: Random House, 1962.

Mayeroff, Milton. "OnCaring," <u>International Philo-sophical Quarterly</u> V (September 1965):462-474.

_____. <u>On Caring</u>. New York: Harper and Row, 1971; Perrenial Library, 1972.

Niebuhr, H. Richard. <u>The Responsible Self</u>. Intro-duction by James M. Gustafson. New York: Harper & Row, 1963.

Polanyi, Michael. <u>Knowing and Being</u>. Edited by Marjorie Grene. Chicago: University of Chicago Press, 1969.

_____. <u>Personal Knowledge</u>. Chicago: University of Chicago Press, 1958, corrected edition, 1962.

_____. <u>Science, Faith and Society</u>. Chicago: University of Chicago Press, 1946.

_____. "Scientific Thought and Social Reality: Essays by Michael Polanyi." Edited by Fred Schwartz. <u>Psychological Issues</u> VIII, Monograph 32. New York: International Universities Press, 1974.

_____. <u>The Study of Man</u>. Chicago: University of Chicago Press, 1959.

_____. <u>The Tacit Dimension</u>. Garden City, New York: Doubleday, 1966, Anchor Books, 1967.

Polanyi, Michael, and Prosch, Harry. <u>Meaning</u>. Chicago: University of Chicago Press, 1975.

Sloan, Douglas, ed. <u>Education and Values</u>. New York: Teachers College Press, 1980.

_____. "Introduction, Knowledge, Education, and Human Values: Toward the Recovery of Wholeness." <u>Teachers College Record</u> 82 (Spring 1981):373-379.

Smith, Huston. "Excluded Knowledge: A Critique of the Western Mind Set." <u>Teachers College Record</u> 80 (February 1979):419-445.

_____. <u>Forgotten Truth</u>. New York: Harper Colophon, 1976.

Smith, John E. <u>Themes in American Philosophy</u>. New York: Harper Torchbooks, 1970.

Thomas, Lewis. "On the Uncertainty of Science."
   Harvard Magazine. (September - October 1980):
   19-22.

Tillich, Paul. The Courage to Be. New Haven: Yale
   University Press, 1952.

Timms, Noel and David Watson, eds. Philosophy in Social
   Work. Boston: Routledge & Kegan Paul, 1978.

Wilkes, Ruth. Social Work with Undervalued Groups.
   London: Tavistock Publications, 1981.

Wilshire, Bruce. "Kierkegaard's Theory of Knowledge
   and New Directions in Psychology and Psychoanalysis." Review of Existential Psychology and Psychiatry III (Fall 1963):249-261.

Wilshire, Donna. "Science and the Dramatic Imagination."
   Performing Arts Review 4 (1973):155-169.

Index

Arendt, Hannah, 17
Aristotle, 18, 139
Art
  and knowledge, 88-9, 91
  and science, 3, 38-9
  and social work, 3
  and mystery, 124
  See also Languages
Ayer, A.J., 72, 75
Barrett, William, 2, 23,
  25, 47, 79, 120, 130, 139
Bartlett, Harriett M., 20,
  140
Behaviorism and Behavior
  Modification, 48-50, 74,
  84
Being
  as prior to knowing,
    120-1
  and hospitality, 123
  and presence, 122
  in social work, 122-4
  and problem solving, 121
Beliefs
  about nature of things,
    137-8
  See also Commitments and
              Science
              Dogmatism
Boehm, Werner W., 18, 140
Bohm, David, 29, 127-8
Bowlby, John, 100
Briar, Scott, and Henry
  Miller, 4, 42-3, 57, 104
British empiricists
  See A.J. Ayer, David Hume
    and John Locke
Bronowski, J., 22, 31, 77,
  95, 112
Broudy, Harry S., 18, 86-7
Buber, Martin, 101-3,
  114-5, 123, 128
Caring, 1, 3-4, 114-6, 138
  and behavior modification,
    49
  and helping, 114
  intervention and
    receptiveness in, 115
  and knowing, 116

as moral principle, 103
  personal growth and, 114
Cartesian dualism, 23
  68-9, 75, 94-5, 136
Cassell, Eric J., 42 110-1
Certainty
  and doubt, 23
  and finitude, 130ff
  and hubris, 29, 120, 143
  and knowledge, 22
  and limitation, 113, 138
  and search for truth, 24
  See also Dogmatism
Charity Organization
  Societies, 5-8, 33-4
Cogito ergo sum, 23, 68
  See also Descartes
Commitments
  in science, 76, 86
Comte, Auguste, 70
Council on Social Work
  Education (CSWE), 10-1
Courage to Be
  See Paul Tillich
Cousins, Norman, 54
Curriculum, Social Work, 11
  values in, 18, 56, 113
Descartes, Rene, 3, 23,
  68-9, 75, 77, 136
Dogmatism, 2-89, 57, 113
  freedom and, 131
  and positivism, 41, 74
  See also Certainty
Effectiveness
  and criticism of practi-
    tioners, 45ff, 73, 141
  cultural context of, 2, 74
  definition of, 43ff, 140
  and supportive treatment,
    53
  Wood study of, 44
  See also Technology and
    Techniques
Einstein, Albert, 76-7
Empiricism
  in philosophy, 68, 94
  in research, 94-5
  limitations of, 103
Encyclopedia of Social Work, 13

151

152

About the Author

Roberta Wells Imre received her Ph.D. in Social Work
from Rutgers University in 1981. She has an MSW from
the Smith College School for Social Work and an M.Div.
from the Yale Divinity School. She lives on Staten
Island in New York and is currently an adjunct assis-
tant professor in the Social Work Department at Seton
Hall University where she has taught and served as
field coordinator. In addition, she has many years
of practice experience, primarily in family agencies
in Michigan and New York.